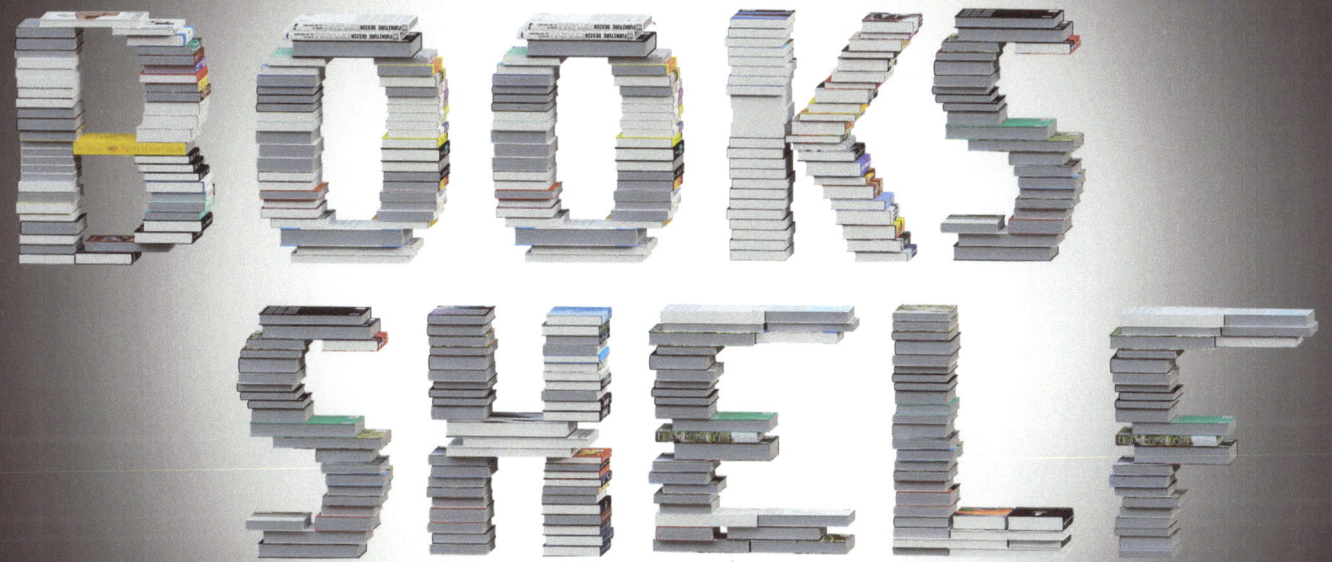

TABLE OF CONTENTS

You want it = we got it

Meet Claudia Clark /author of "Dear Barack" **3 - 4**

A Short Story By Tara September **5 - 6**

Meet Michele Baker /author of "All we need is Love" **7 -8**

A Short Story by Paula D. Tozer **9 -10**

Meet Sylvia Greif /author of "Ela Green and the Kingdom of Abud" **11 -14**

An excerpt from Circles, Lines, and Squiggles by by W. Nikola-Lisa **15 -16**

Meet Kristen James /author of "The Billionaire who bought Me" **17 -20**

Meet Loni Lynne /author of "Immortal Heat"/   21 - 24

Meet author Jody Hadlock   25

Meet author Joy Harding   26

Meet author Glenn Goodwin   27

Meet author Josie Malone   28

Meet author Sheldon Shalley   29

Meet author Melissa Cynova   30 - 31

Meet author T. L. Scott   32 - 33

Meet author D.K. Marie   34

DEAR BARACK

THE EXTRAORDINARY PARTNERSHIP OF BARACK OBAMA AND ANGELA MERKEL
by Claudia Clark

A Non-fiction account of the eight year working partnership between former U.S. President and former German Chancellor Angela Merkel

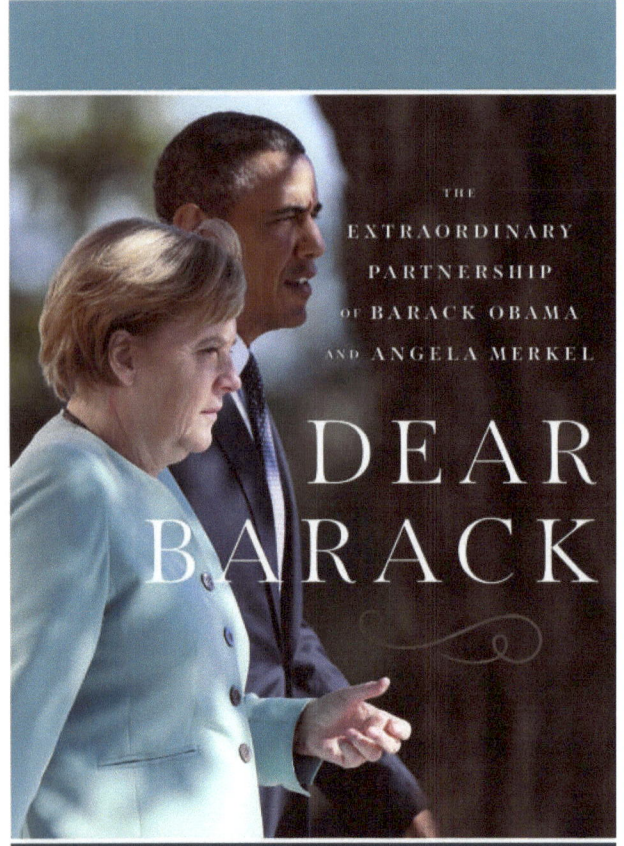

Today, we know US President Barack Obama and German Chancellor Angela Merkel as two of the world's most influential leaders, together at the center of some of the biggest controversies and most impressive advancements of our time. But while their friendship has been the subject of both scrutiny and admiration, few know the full story.

Taking office at the height of the 2008 global recession, Obama was keenly aware of the fractured relationship between the US and Europe. And for her part, Merkel was suspicious of the charismatic newcomer who had captivated her country.

Faced with the challenges of globalization, the two often clashed over policy, but—as the first Black president and first female chancellor—they shared a belief that democracy could uplift the world. United by this conviction, they would forge a complicated but inspiring partnership.

Dear Barack is a thoroughly researched document of the parallel trajectories that led to Obama and Merkel meeting on the world stage and the trials, both personal and political, that they confronted in office. At times in the leaders' own words, the book details such events as Merkel's historic acceptance of the Presidential Medal of Freedom, Russia's annexation of Crimea, and the 2013 NSA spying scandal, demonstrating the highs and lows of this extraordinary alliance.

A story of camaraderie at a global scale, Dear Barack shows that it is possible for political adversaries to establish bonds of respect—and even friendship—in the service of the free world.

"Clark's book retells a fascinating and necessary chapter of U.S. relations with Germany. Dear Barack is a reminder that the U.S. can always return to the era of Obama and Merkel's companionship, and that the world would be a better place if it did." —Shari Temple, Democrats Abroad Germany Voting Representative and 2008 DNC Obama delegate

Claudia Clark
AUTHOR OF "DEAR BARACK"

I am an American feminist/political activist living in Berlin. My debut book, Dear Barack: The extraordinary partnership of Barack Obama and Angela Merkel was published in both English and German in the fall of 2021.

Barack Obama and Angela Merkel, two of the most influential leaders of the twenty first century forged an unlikely and deep bond that captivated the world.

At times in the leaders' own words, the book details such events as Merkel's historic acceptance of the Presidential Medal of Freedom, Russia's annexation of Crimea, and the 2013 NSA spying scandal, demonstrating the highs and lows of this extraordinary alliance.

Obama and Merkel often disagreed on important policy decisons, but in effort to uphold the promise of democracy, they placed their differences aside for the betterment of the western world. A lesson other

What's the dream? Whom would you like to be as big as?

Slince I wrote my book on the relationship between Obama and Merkel, my dream would be to meet them in person(ideally at the same time) and talk to them about the book and get their insights.

We all know the writer's path is never easy, what makes you keep going? What advice would you give to new authors?

Stand firm in your conviction. Unfortunately the publishing field is very competitive and you are going to get a lot of rejection and a lot of the rejection is flat out rude and unneccessary. It can be discouraging, but if you believe in what you are doing then don't let the rejection and negativity get to you.

IT MIGHT BE YOU

A Short Story By Tara September

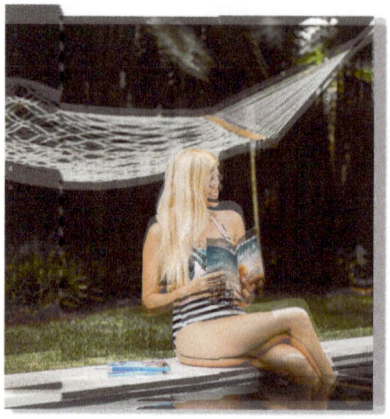

So, this was her new and exciting life in Florida?

Serina Spring sighed and tossed down her losing hand of cards. On a sunny Wednesday afternoon in one of Florida's most beautiful cities, here she was, playing Michigan Rummy with a rowdy group of octogenarians.

"There she goes," her spritely but aging Nana, called out triumphantly. "The girls and I are coming for you."

'The girls' were all widowed, and, at the moment, talking a lot of smack as they goaded one another over a pot full of pennies. Given their furrowed brows of concentration and groans of defeat, you would think they were playing for a new Cadillac.

She'd learned how to play the card game during her childhood visits to her great-grandmother's home in Naples, Florida and often joined their lively game whenever she was in town.

The curly-haired Carolyn collected one of the larger pots of the day, drawing the winnings to her side of the table with a goofy giggle. "How long are you visiting us this time, dear?"

"Indefinitely! I'm relocating permanently," Her news stirred up a round of excited squeals from the group and a cackle from Carolyn. "I'm rooming here with Nana, but I hope to have my own place soon, once I am settled in with work."

"What will you do for a living?"

"The same as I did in Manhattan. Lucky for me, it's a good time to be selling real estate in Naples." That was true. Serina had done her homework before moving. "With houses for sale in excess of $40 million, Southwest Florida is the most expensive market in the country right now."

These were the same figures she'd recited when her single friends and former colleagues told her she was crazy for leaving the thrill of New York City and her burgeoning career there to start anew. Sure, she was essentially starting over, but the prospect of a clean slate thrilled her more than it daunted. She was eager to start building her Naples portfolio and get a better lay of the land.

"Of course, the median sale is about $250,000, but hey, a girl could dream, no?"

"That's right." Nana beamed with pride. "She passed the Florida Real Estate Broker Examination with ease and tomorrow is her first day at a fancy agency."

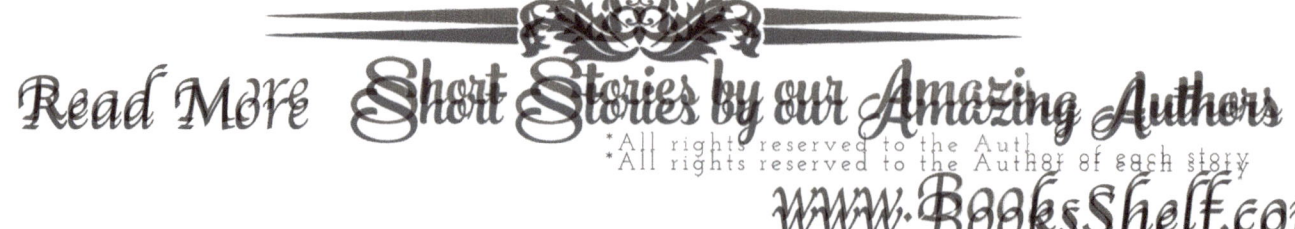

*All rights reserved to the Author of each story

www.BooksShelf.com

"Is your fella going to move down here too?" Nana's friend, Helen Montgomery asked wistfully.

"Uh…" Serina fumbled for a response. She was still getting used to the idea that her fella preferred other fellas.

"That didn't work out," Nana broke in, gently patting Serina's non-card playing hand, which was currently wadded into a fist.

Helen gasped as if she'd just lost her own boyfriend of three years. "But with your lovely rich brown hair and slender figure, you're a dead ringer for your Nana here when she was younger. Lord knows she had to beat them away with a stick. Actually, I was just telling Junior that you look like a modern-day Natalie Wood."

Serina always liked Helen the best out of Nana's cronies.

The sour-faced Ann, on the other hand tutted. "Thirty and still single."

Yup, she'd just turned thirty at the same time her boyfriend, Justin, had turned gay. Well, she supposed he had always been gay. He'd just finally had the guts to tell her.

Surprise!

Justin prided himself on being a wonderful gift-giver and his recent declaration was definitely the biggest birthday surprise she had ever had. It just wasn't the kind of icing on her birthday cake she'd been expecting. No, she had foolishly expected an engagement ring to celebrate the occasion.

In hindsight, there had been signs. Serina even used to worry that he spent a little too much time at an all-male gym, was meticulously tidy, and that, maybe, just maybe, their relationship felt forced. Regardless, she needed space to cope with the revelation. Seven states of space, to be exact.

Plus, she was tired of the Manhattan rat race. She had worked non-stop at her agency during the day, answering her clients' demanding calls and texts at all hours of the night. The mere thought of jumping back into the dating pool again in that cement jungle left her feeling exhausted. And with winter being in full swing, it made her decision to move south all the more appealing.

Looking out over the small lake beyond Nana's screened lanai, Serina took a deep breath, soaking in the balmy seventy-five-degree weather. Sinking her body into the wicker chair, the tension left her tight shoulders immediately.

This is paradise.

Keep Reading on BooksShelf.com

Books by Tara September

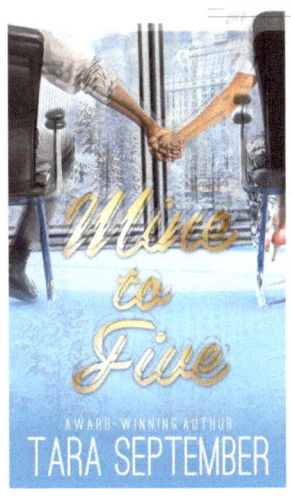
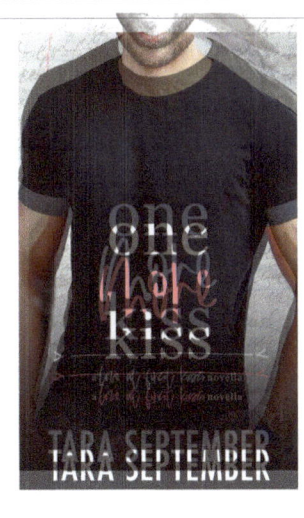
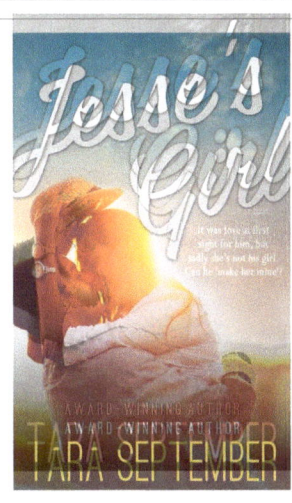
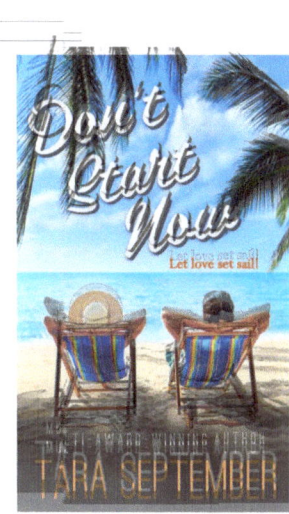

All We Need Is Love
IN SERVICE TO THE LIGHT (BOOK ONE)

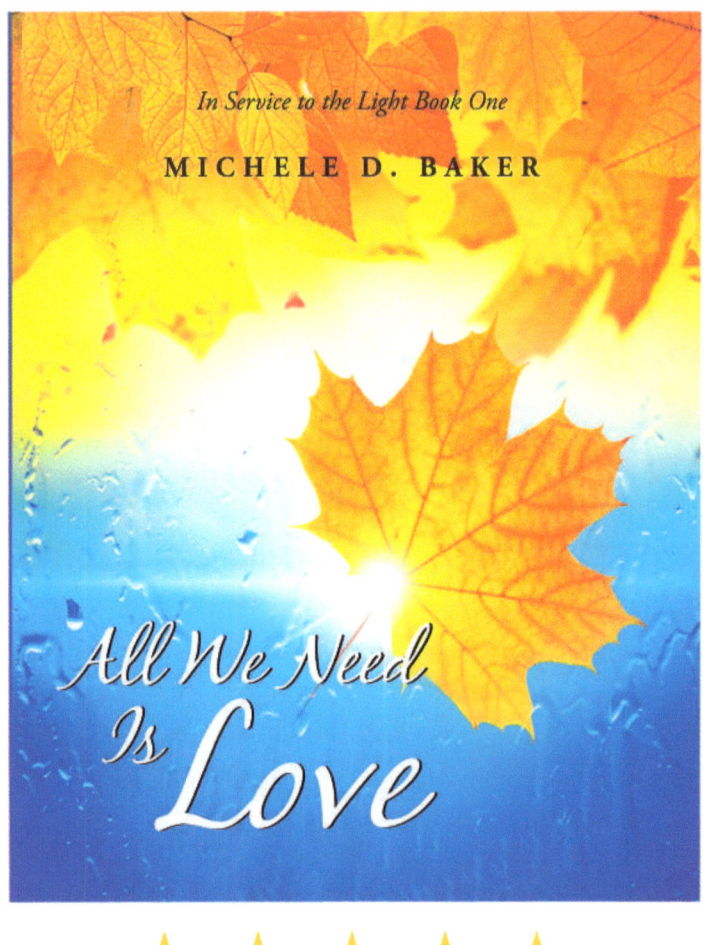

In Service to the Light Book One

MICHELE D. BAKER

★★★★★

"Love is all that is needed
Michele's connection with Archangel Michael is profound and filled with spiritual knowledge of the transition from 3rd to the 5th Dimension. Her book explains in a relaxed and humorous manner the changes that are happening right now."

"ANGELIC EXPERIENCE
MIchele's insight provided a richly rewarding experience into a world most people do not know exists. Once you become part of the experience, you want to continue the journey with great anticipation for what comes next. The author's prose was poetic and angelic. I hope we are rewarded with another novel from this talented writer."

Taken from her diary of channeled messages, Michele offers insights from this world and beyond to comfort, encourage, and inspire each of us to simply relax and enjoy the ride. "All We Need Is Love," because we are who we have been waiting for!

Are you feeling overwhelmed? Confused? Do you wake up tired and simply drag through your day, wondering if this is all there is? Maybe you feel that the whole world is going down the tubes... everything from relationships, to education, to politics and money. Just what is going on around here?

"All We Need Is Love" offers a simple explanation for what is happening all around us. The whole planet, and every being on it, is ascending to a higher level of consciousness! For that to happen, the old ways, the old ideas, and the old systems must break down and clear away.

Far from going down the tubes, we are all on the brink of something much, much better. Since you are here at this time in history, you are part of that grand awakening... even more, you are already perfectly equipped to handle this transition.

Taken from her diary of channeled messages, Michele offers insights from this world and beyond to comfort, encourage, and inspire each of us to simply relax and enjoy the ride. All we need is love, because we are who we have been waiting for.

MICHELE BAKER

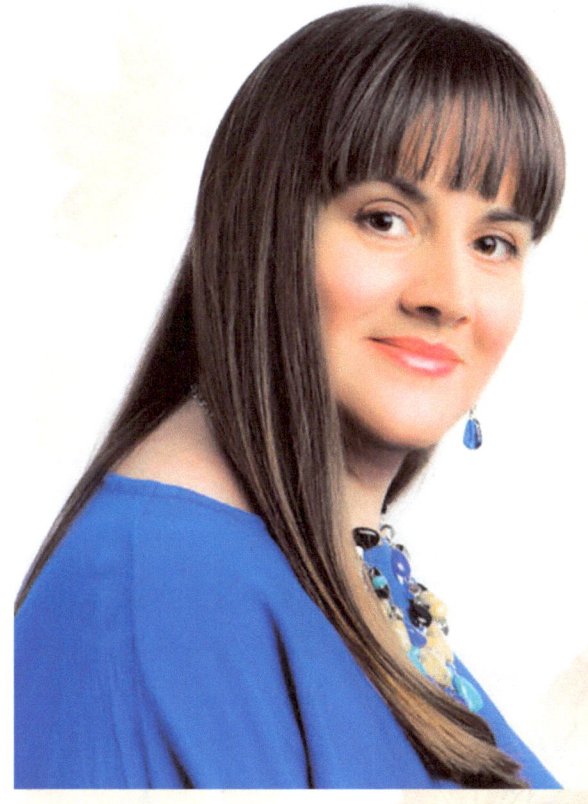

At heart, I'm basically a writer. My love of the written word began when I was a little girl, when I used to fold in half and staple together notebook paper to create little books.

As I got older, and attended college and then massage school, it was clear that my written assignments - whether they were essays on Milton or haiku poems for English class, book reports, or even written proofs of Calculus problems - attracted the bulk of my attention. My passion was nurtured in those sentences, those phrases, and each week brought new opportunities to practice my craft.

I've always been an avid reader, too - I believe all writers are. We read to get ideas, to soak up language, to dwell in that deep imagination space where creativity is birthed and grows, building and expanding until it overflows onto the page (or the screen, as the case may be). I am also an avid collector of quotes, both inspirational and educational, and my literary heroes are Ken Carey, Dr. Wayne Dyer, and William Blake.

In my late thirties, I discovered I could hear and talk to Angelic beings, and through the automatic writing in my journal, I began recording extraordinary information about the future of the planet. After a reluctant start, I have now joyfully accepted my assigned task and am thrilled to be spreading these exciting and life-changing messages in "All We Need Is Love: In Service to the Light Book One (available now in print, e-book and audiobook formats) and the forthcoming "Attitude of Gratitude: In Service to the Light Book Two!

Angelo's Stigmata by Paula D. Tozer

Everywhere in the city, he could see the signs of spring. Pigeons, small finches, and red-breasted robins hunted for a meal in the vacant lots and in the parks. The snow had melted and all that remained were oily puddles drying in the naked sunshine.

Angelo sat on a bench at the edge of a ballfield, the warmth of the sun on his back. A few hundred yards away some children had taken up a game. He could hear them laughing and shouting. A few words. Names. Taunts. Excited screams when one of them got a home run.

Angelo enjoyed the game from where he sat; he wouldn't think of going over there and scaring them away. He was uncomfortable when he thought about looking frightening to children. It was something he tried very hard not to do. He dressed neatly. He was always careful not to smell.

His dark gray overcoat had been worn under the arms and at the elbows by one of the old men at the boarding house. It was his now. His dark green work pants were too long, covering his black rubber overshoes. Too big for the sneakers he wore underneath, they slapped the concrete as he shuffled along.

Angelo's appearance hid many secrets. Most people didn't come close enough to look into his warm brown eyes. He didn't tell anyone about the large wooden cross that hung suspended under his clothes by a red knotted lanyard. Father Bob gave it to him after mass one Sunday. Angelo held it in his hands as he prayed for the poor people of the city. He prayed because he saw their hurt and tears formed in his eyes as he remembered them all. Especially Belinda.

His mother taught him to love, how to pray, and how to look after himself.

Life can be hard, she told him. It is like living in a tidy house or a messy house – it takes effort every day to keep it neat. His mother told him these things when she was sitting quietly after supper, watching the news. He remembered her gray hair that was slightly tinted with blue and her bangs that she cut square across her forehead. He could see her legs slightly apart and she was fanning herself with a scribbler because it was hot in the house. It was summertime and they didn't have any air conditioning. Not even a fan. Angelo remembered sweating and listening to her above the voice of the announcer on the television. His mother liked to talk to him after supper.

She said the thing with messes is that they don't go away. Look at those dishes. I dirtied them making supper. They are just lying there waiting for me to clean them up. It is the same thing with mistakes – you do dirt to someone you are responsible for making it right. Angelo, you will have to do the cleaning, she said.

It wasn't until after she died, and Roma let him live in the small attic room of the boarding house where the pigeons roost that he understood what his mother had told him.

Angelo had no one to tell him she loved him. He felt lost and alone and hid in his room until the day he remembered that she said another thing. He had to become his own mother and father and be a man of honor.

Working through his loneliness, Angelo remembered something else she had taught him. A reminder of this now hung around his neck, and peace surrounded him as he went about his day.

Okay, he thought. It's okay.

It was late morning and the children had given up on the game. They parted ways, each running their own path out of the park. Angelo groaned as he roused himself and began shuffling down the street.

Lunchtime at the soup kitchen. Angelo couldn't have put words on the things he saw, the people he talked to, the ones he reached for and patted on the shoulder, helped with their coats and rumpled garbage bags. But he felt what they felt as they put their belongings into those bags with care reserved for precious cargo.

Old men coughing. Faded females. Dry bony fingers, yellow-stained, reaching uncertainly for salt, crackers. Shaking hands squeezing the plastic cracker package before opening it and crumbling it into thin amber soup. He could smell the death that clung to their skin and clothes. He loved them all – the cautious, the guarded. The whining ones. The sullen ones. The sick ones who coughed bright and bloody into stolen toilet paper.

He would pull up a chair beside each one; those he called his friends. Not the ones who spat on him and called him "freak" and pulled their children close to them. Sometimes they would hit him.

He would ask his friends about their day. After their meal, he would take out his matches and light their cigarettes and his eyes would roam their faces as they talked, and he smiled. As he helped them prepare to leave, he would offer his thick, rough hand in farewell.

Gentlemen shake hands, his mother told him. Believe the words you speak, and others will believe them, she said. Be a man of conviction. It was what his mother and father-self told him every day.

The kitchen crew was peeling potatoes for supper when Angelo left the soup kitchen. The afternoon sun was warm and bright. He squinted and felt in his pants pocket for his money.

Angelo received a pension. Roma looked after his rent and his food and gave him spending money. At Joe's grocery store across the street, he bought a single large orange. The kind from far away, with the little sticker on it. They were always sweet and juicy. Angelo smiled as he thought of the old woman enjoying it.

He walked the several blocks to her home, greeting people and smiling. Sometimes he cringed from what he saw. Freddie was there, sitting on the stoop in front of his apartment. Freddie always cursed him and threw trash. He crossed the street and Freddie hardly noticed him at all.

Angelo knew his mind wasn't sharp. He understood that he would never marry or have children. You look different, Angelo, his mother said. Sometimes people will be mean to you because you have that look. Show them your heart anyway. Your heart is as strong as any man.

Keep Reading on BooksShelf.com

BOOKS BY PAULA D. TOZER

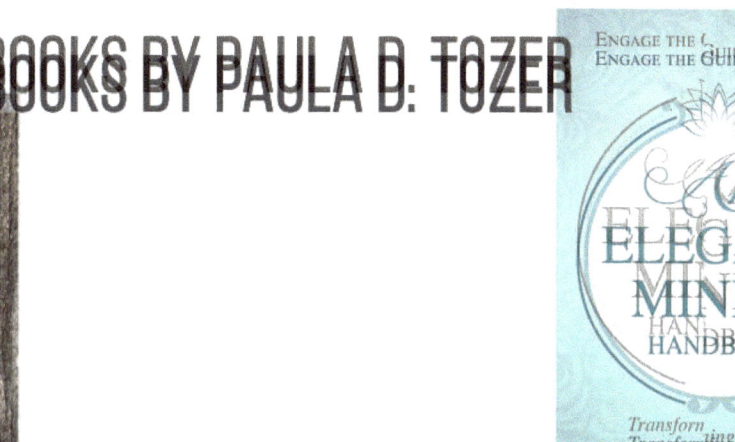

SYLVIA GREIF

SWISS WRITER, SINGER AND ANIMAL ADVOCATE

"I am at my happiest in the great outdoors, playing sports. I walked part of the Way of Santiago in 2018 and I hope to climb Mount Kilimanjaro in the near future.

My passion for the environment and wildlife started when I was a child.
I grew up surrounded by pets and all kinds of animals and It always felt they were part of my family. I believe they have shaped me, and the compassion and respecttowards them Is without a doubt deeply
instilled in me.

I work alongside non-profit organisations to protect animal rights, and fight animal cruelty. I have three dogs, BV, Shea and Lola.

In 2014 I released a children's book , Lester's Planet, that tells the story with a paw of imagination, of a little chihuahua with a bottomless
stomach."

Ela Green and the Kingdom of Abud is my first novel in a trilogy and introduces Ela Green, a fourteen-year-old girl. Her first adventure reveals the mysterious bond she shares with Mother Nature and her encounter with the wise-tree.

The adventure starts in the present day at Waldegg boarding school on the shores of lake Geneva in Switzerland .The formidable school is the connecting link in a story that will time-travel you through continents and centuries."

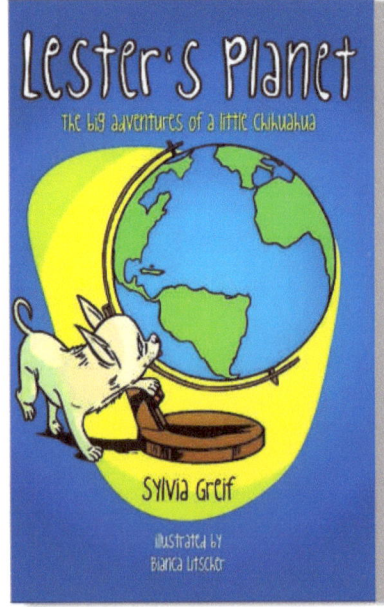
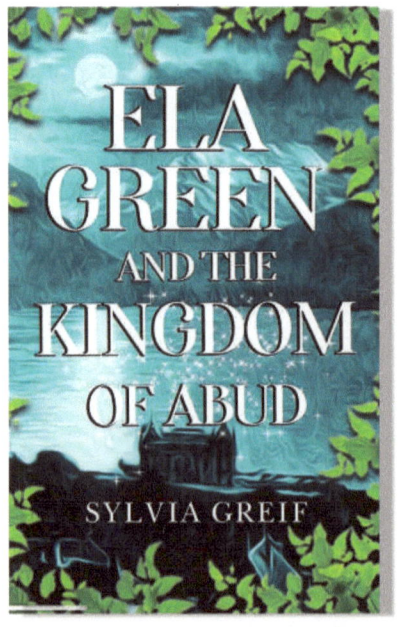

Sylvia G, formerly Milow The Girl, has led an unusual life. The Swiss artist grew up surrounded by lion cubs, chimpanzees, a baby elephant and a menagerie of exotic wildlife. She travelled the world from a young age, and is fluent in six languages. Her love for animals goes back as far as she can remember, but her venture into music came much later.

Her singing career started in 2007 when her song Waking Up received the award for Best Dance Track at the USA Songwriting Competition. The award helped her to secure live performances at high profile festivals and venues including the Montreux Jazz Festival (Switzerland), the Shanghai International Music Festival (China), Le Reservoir Club (Paris), and the Whiskey A Go-Go (Los Angeles). Two years later she received the award for Best European Singer at the LA Music Awards.

In 2010 she signed to US based label Realize Records. That same year the label released her debut album Days of Power, recorded in Miami with French producer Charlie Nestor. Joe Jackson's guitarist Vinnie Zummo collaborated on some of the tracks.

Her second album 32,000 Feet Above was released in 2012. The album was recorded in Nashville and Los Angeles with award winning producer Robert Venable (former Evanescence drummer, and producer of Megadeth and INXS). It features musicians Kendra Chantelle (American Idol), Thad Beaty (Beyonce, Sugarland), and rapper Kuf Knotz, and produced several successful singles including Beautiful World and Distraction. In 2013 Milow The Girl partnered with Right Recordings to release the single Distraction, remixed by Timothy Allan and Loverush. The song went on to reach Number 14 on the Music Week Commercial Pop Chart.

In February 2015 Milow The Girl's third album Overexposed was one of the most streamed indie releases, with nearly a million streams worldwide. The album was recorded in Los Angeles and London with producers/songwriters Robert Venable, Keaton Simons and Stuart Epps.

The album Dreams, recorded in 2016, was co-written and produced in Los Angeles by Josh Ricchio. The title track, a remix of the Fleetwood Mac hit, stays true to the original but with its own unique sound. The album reached Number 2 in the US Adult Contemporary downloads charts and Number 1 on the Adult Contemporary streaming chart.

Following the success of Dreams, Sylvia G recorded her fifth studio album SOS in London, with Uk based label Right Recordings.

In April 2021 her uplifting new single Smile was released.

Her New album due out May 2022.

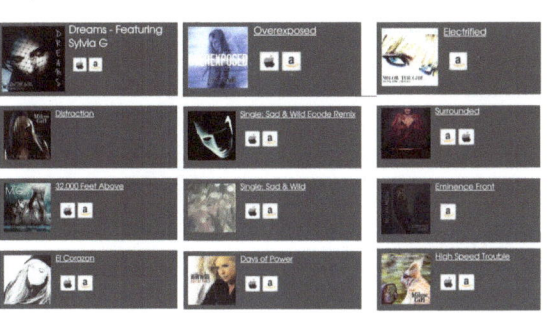

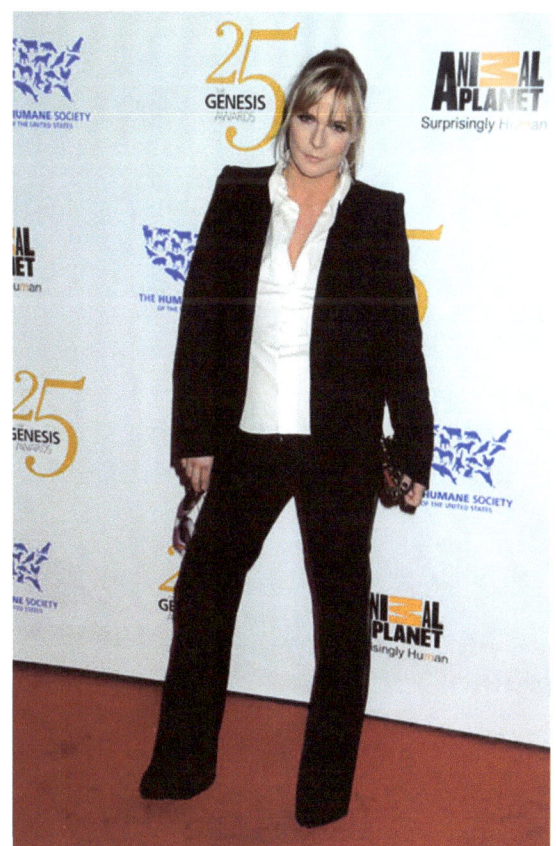

LESTER'S PLANET
LESTER'S SECRET
The big adventures of a little Chihuahua

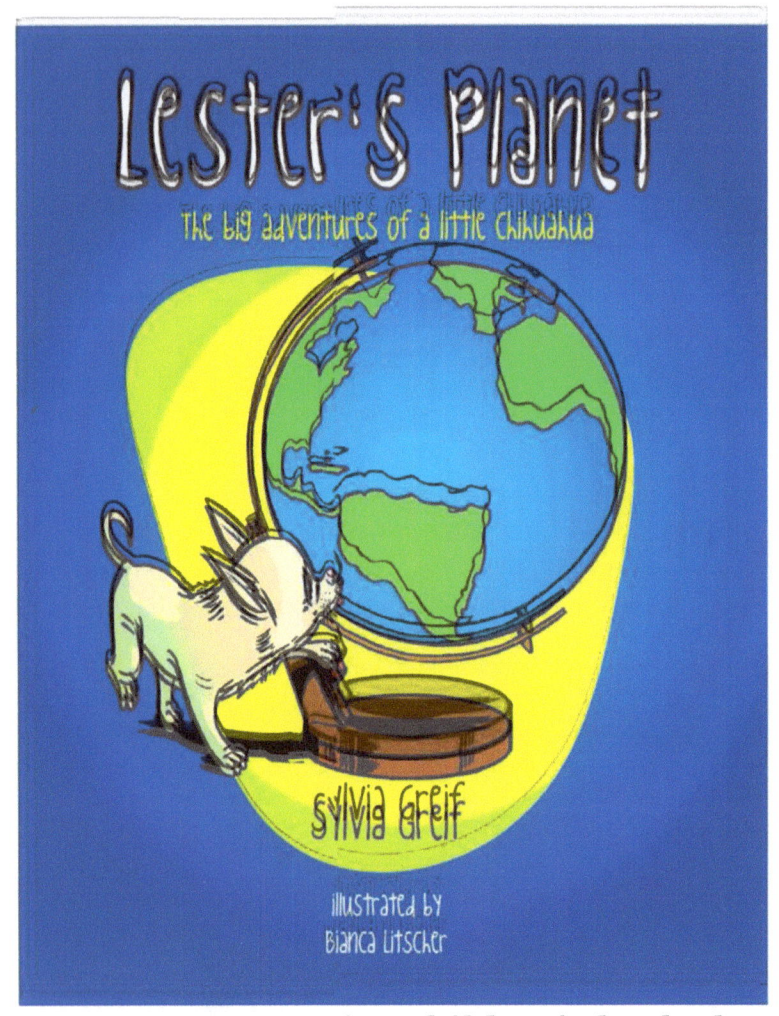

Everyone meet Lester. This little Chihuahua with the bottomless stomach is full of energy and excitement. It's a good thing he is adopted by international singing sensation Marie Ailvys, because she loves adventure. And this begins a story that travels across the globe filled with adventures and mysteries. Along the way, Lester and Marie encounter many other dogs in search of loving families. Lester's secret is the origin story about Lester's and Marie's relationship, his trip across Europe and North America, and the wonderful secret he has:

A fun and engaging children's book about the little Chihuahua Lester, and his big adventures around the world! Full of positivity, life lessons, and beautiful written adventure!

This book is based on a true story with a paw of imagination and tells the story of a little chihuahua named Lester.

We hope you enjoy it as much as Sylvia and Bianca enjoyed writing and drawing his first adventure!

Ela Green AND THE KINGDOM OF ABUD

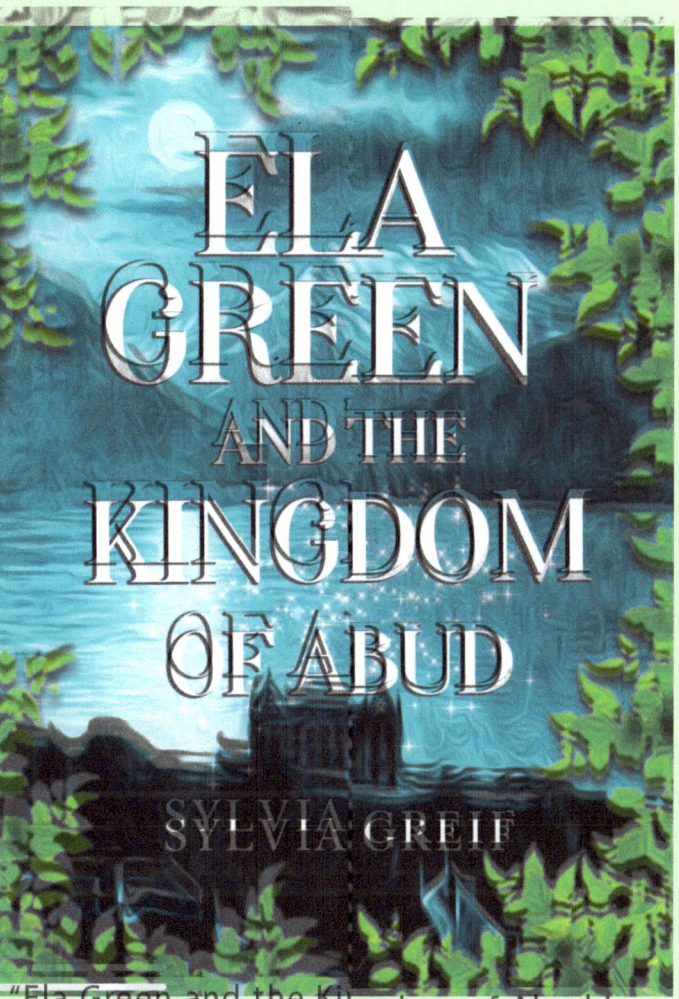

Ela Green and the Kingdom of Abud is book one of a trilogy and introduces Ela Green, a fourteen-year-old girl. Her first adventure reveals the mysterious bond she shares with Mother Nature and her encounter with Yggdrasil, the wise-tree, charting her own self-discovery along the way. With the help of her best friend, Jo, and her loving Uncle Archibald, who unwillingly has to lay bare an unbelievable secret, Ela summons all her courage to face the many dangers along the road.

The adventure starts in the present day at Waldegg Boarding School on the shores of Lake Geneva in Switzerland. As Mrs. Green drives her daughter back after the summer holidays, Ela has no idea that the discovery of an ancient bracelet and a scroll she found in an antique desk will change her life forever.

The formidable school is the connecting link in an adventure that will time-travel the reader through continents and centuries in search of the mysterious kingdom and the magical Book of Name, the most powerful manuscript ever written...

And for a prophecy that must be fulfilled.

"Ela Green and the Kingdom of Abud is my first novel in a trilogy and introduces Ela Green, a fourteen-year-old girl. Her first adventure reveals the mysterious bond she shares with Mother Nature and her encounter with the wise-tree.

The adventure starts in the present day at Waldegg boarding school on the shores of lake Geneva in Switzerland. The formidable school is the connecting link in a story that will time-travel you through continents and centuries."

Sylvia Greif

AN EXCERPT FROM CIRCLES, LINES, AND SQUIGGLES: Astrology for the Curious-Minded

BY W. NIKOLA-LISA

When we think of the symbolic nature of numbers, several numbers come immediately to mind: 1, 3, 4, 7, 9, and 12, with each number carrying a set of associations based on their numerical properties. Of the six, the number twelve holds several unique qualities. First of all, it is the number of greatest magnitude that, in English, has just one syllable. Numerically, it is the smallest composite number with exactly six divisors (1, 2, 3, 4, 6, and 12). It is also the smallest abundant number, a number for which the sum of its proper divisors is greater than itself (2 + 3 + 4 + 6 = 16). Moreover, the number twelve is a sublime number, which is a positive integer with a perfect number of positive factors, all of which add up to form another perfect number. In the case of twelve, we have: 1 + 2 + 3 + 4 + 6 +12 = 28. Sublime numbers are very rare, so twelve, being one of them and the smallest sublime number to boot, makes this number quite special.2 Finally, twelve appears in most calendar systems—solar and lunar—and is deeply implicated in the nature of time. A year has twelve months. An analog clock has twelve hours, serving both ante meridiem (a.m.) and post meridiem (p.m.) hours. Additionally, the basic units of time—60 minutes or 60 seconds—are evenly divisible by twelve and its divisors. Aside from its mathematical qualities, what does the number twelve represent symbolically?

Castor: Haven't a clue.

Pollux: When I think about a clock, I think about a circle that is continuously moving, never ending.

Castor: Until the battery stops.

Author: I like the image of a continuously moving object. It suggests a sense of balance, a sense of wholeness and completion. It also suggests a sense of history and tradition, as well as a sense of authority, at least that's what most of the occult literature says. Perhaps this is why the number twelve appears repeatedly as an organizational principle of countless civilizations, especially in the ancient and classical world. Is it a coincidence that there are twelve Olympians in Greek mythology? Mythic by nature, but all-too-human in their petty jealousies and insecurities, the twelve Olympians are at once real and symbolic, a mirror held up to the ancient Greeks to help them understand the chaos of the world around them. But why twelve Olympians? Why not ten, or eleven, or thirteen for that matter? The same could be said about one of the most legendary heroes of Greco-Roman lore, Hercules. Why, after killing his wife and children in a fit of madness, a madness brought on by Hera, Zeus's jealous wife and Hercules's mother, was Hercules condemned to complete twelve labors imposed by his older brother Eurystheus, whom he served? Why not seven labors, or eight, or sixteen?

Castor: I never really thought about it.

Author: The number twelve didn't surface only in ancient myths and stories. It had a presence in the everyday organization of society. For purposes of self-preservation, cities often formed into confederations or leagues. This should not be surprising. However, the confederations were often composed of twelve regional cities. The most important league during the early Greco-Roman era was the Etruscan League (though "Leagues" is more appropriate, since there were several confederations that extended from the foothills of the Alps to the Amalfi coast). Like other leagues, it was a "dodecapolis," a federation of twelve autonomous cities bound together by trade and military alliance.3 Why twelve? Again, why not six, or ten, or fourteen? Was it a coincidence, a geographic convenience, or was it symbolic of something else, something greater?

Pollux: A geographic convenience.

Castor: Naw, a coincidence.

Author: I side with "symbolic of something greater." Along with suggesting completion and wholeness, the number twelve also suggests equality and cohesion. At the same time, the number twelve suggests differentiation from the outside world: internal cohesion and differentiation from others—two essential ingredients for a successful alliance in an uncertain and hostile world. Although the Etruscan League disappeared as Etruscan civilization was absorbed into the ever-expanding Roman empire, the number twelve didn't disappear. Instead, it found a place in Roman rule and law, in the Law of the Twelve Tables, otherwise known as the Duodecim Tabulae, a set of laws inscribed on twelve bronze tablets that appeared in ancient Rome around 451-450 BCE.4 According to the Roman statesman and scholar Cicero, they just didn't appear: they were ceremoniously placed in the Roman Forum for all of Rome's citizens to read. The Duodecim Tabulae became the de facto basis of Roman law, binding both patrician (aristocrat) and plebeian (commoner) together in one codified legal system. Though not a comprehensive code of laws, it was one of the earliest instances in which a government drew up, posted, and enforced a set of laws common to its citizens. But why twelve bronze tablets?

Castor: I know, why not four, or seven, or ten?

Author: In fact, there were ten tablets originally.

Castor: Just what I thought.

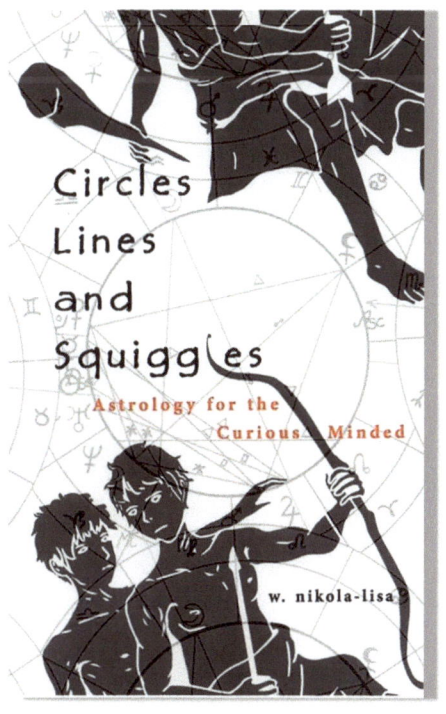

02 The Billionaire who bought Me
BY KRISTEN JAMES

"Looking for a female companion; not what you think but it pays very well."

Could I do it? I needed A LOT of money to help my sister stay alive until she could get a heart transplant. Maybe this was the answer.

Zoe Montgomery is intrigued by the ad that promises a lot of money for a few weeks of her time—if she makes it to the end. She's desperate, but the ad is vague. What will he want from her? His ad mentions travel and "no touching" so what else does he want? She finds the billionaire behind the words just as mysterious and confusing, breaking all her conceived ideas and toying with her emotions. She also discovers the rules in their ruse are made to be broken. Will she make it the full two weeks and get her big payday? And will it be enough money to save her little sister?

So I hit the link and a few seconds later I was staring at a well-dressed man, but I blinked, worried that I had ended up in the wrong Zoom meeting.

Wow. Not what I expected at all.

For starters, he looked around 30. He was much closer to my age than what I'd expected. He was stunningly handsome with thick hair, a chiseled face, and brown eyes that looked curious and full of energy. It wasn't until that second that I realized I had been picturing an older man who wasn't handsome at all. It unsettled me. Was this better? Worse? Calm as cold steel, he openly studied me.

Again I wondered, why did he choose me to interview? He was young, hot, and rich, and he wanted to talk to me.

Wait a sec, why did he need to hire someone? He was gorgeous.

Leighton Forester

They say the perfect woman doesn't exist, but those people didn't realize you can create her. Well, if you have enough money. I started by knowing exactly what I needed, and then running an ad, and finding someone who could mold herself into my model woman.

Zoe was working out better than I could have anticipated, at least thus far. She didn't have a big Instagram following or some other influencer profile. The other girls had all been trying to build an online platform and even thought they could use this job as a way to do that. So the choice had been quick and easy.

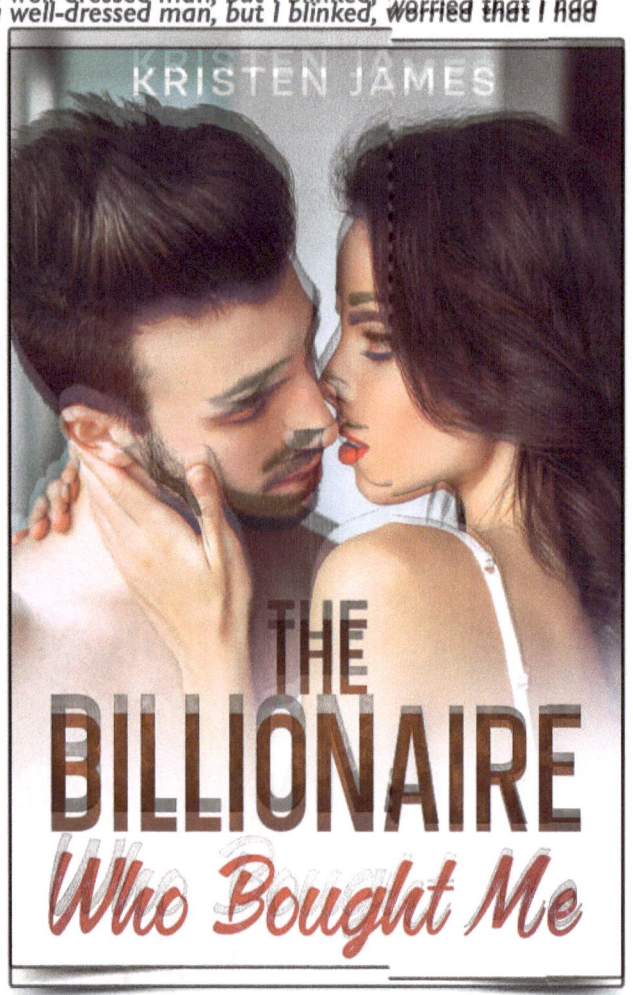

Actually, it'd been almost too easy. She was the only one I felt any kind of interest in.

I had known I would have to feel some attraction to whoever I hired for this to work, and now I found that I had to ignore that. But, the ball was rolling. I would just have to get through this.

The Interview
A short story BY KRISTEN JAMES

Breathe in... one two three. Breathe out... one two three.

Nova Elliot closed her eyes as she counted her slow breaths. She stood on the balcony outside her marketing firm's building. Thankfully none of the smokers or vapor users were here, which would trigger her asthma.

For now she had the quaint little balcony overlooking a small corner of the park to herself. Tiny yellow birds chirped in the giant tree that stretched over her building's roof. The late morning sun came through the treetop in spots.

The breeze tickled over her arms and through her long, red hair. It was casual Friday at work but she still wore a black blazer over a floral top paired with skinny jeans and low heeled boots. She had to stay sharp all the time, and that included looking like she was here ready to work.

She wanted to enjoy the picturesque setting, but it was time to get back at it, even though she didn't feel as relaxed as she normally did after her breathing break. She sighed and swung the door open, walking down the hallway toward the lobby and her corner office at the other end. The office had been a way to placate her instead of a real promotion and raise, and it had an ugly view of an intersection below.

I like my job. I like my job. I like my job.

And, she was next in line for the position opening up above her. She had waited two years for it, proving herself over and over. Finally, it was all but official. Out of everyone at her office, she brought in the most clients and had the highest return on investment for her marketing campaigns.

Halfway to her office, she spotted someone waiting in the empty lobby. A nicely dressed man sat on the sofa, gazing at the oversized abstract artwork on the wall. It was trendy but she didn't care for abstract. The man, however, was very nice to look at.

Long and well-built, he had a relaxed air about him. He wore a cashmere sweater in baby blue with tan slacks. He looked to be around her age with blond, almost curly hair that was perfectly styled. His put-together style made her think he was from another firm, although she wasn't sure why.

He glanced at her with gorgeous hazel eyes, set off even more by his baby blue sweater. All in all, a very nice package, like he could the model for sweater ad. Was that why he was here?

Her mind had been preoccupied and it was a surprise to find someone so good looking sitting there. She liked to think that she didn't put so much weight on a person's appearance but she couldn't stop staring. It took her a few seconds to react properly.

"Can I help you?" she asked, smiling in case it was a client. She still didn't think so. Clients usually had appointments and they tried not to make anyone wait. That was why this felt like an unplanned visit.

He returned her smile, flashing dimples and white teeth. Lord help her.

"Hello, I'm Elliot Arlington. I'm here for the interview."

Interview?

"Oh?" She went blank, cringing in her mind for showing her surprise. To cover, she said, "I'll let them know you're here. I'm not sure where Isabel is."

She avoided eye contact as she went behind the receptionist's desk to call her boss, but Rick came down the hallway before she could. His office overlooked the park, of course.

"Elliot, welcome!" Rick said, waving him back. The two men greeted each other like old friends, but their words said otherwise. Her boss avoided her eyes as Elliot walked back to his door.

She stood there, still in shock. What position could he be interviewing for? And why wasn't Isabel at her desk at eleven in the morning? Ironically, Isabel appeared then too.

"Hi Nova!" she chirped, bustling in. "Did you need something?"
"Oh, I was helping a man here for an interview. Do you know what that's about?"

Isabel sat in her chair and gazed up at Nova with big brown eyes—eyes that were overly blank and innocent right now.

"Oh really? No, I don't know."
"Oh, well." Nova gave a laugh like it wasn't anything important. "Is everything alright with you?"

It probably sounded like a strange question, but she was curious why Isabel had been gone when there was a scheduled interview. Maybe she hadn't known?

"Oh, Rick asked me to take some files down to illustration." She turned back to her computer and started typing.

Nova went back to her office, trying not to assume that Rick had sent the receptionist away so he could sneak Elliot in for an interview. It would have been easier to send her on a fool's errand so she wouldn't see.
There was only one position that would be open soon... Rick had told her they wouldn't interview outside the firm, that that job was all but hers.
Or had he actually promised it? Pacing in her small space, she tried to remember his words to see if he'd danced around an actual commitment. She couldn't recall. They'd spoken numerous times, and she had felt sure the job was hers.
She breathed, counting, pacing, and then finally just watching the traffic below. That had completely ruffled her. That Elliot guy was off the cute scale and also super friendly, although that hadn't even been a conversation. But to find out he was interviewing for her promotion? She couldn't believe Rick would do that to her, again!

Keep Reading on BooksShelf.com

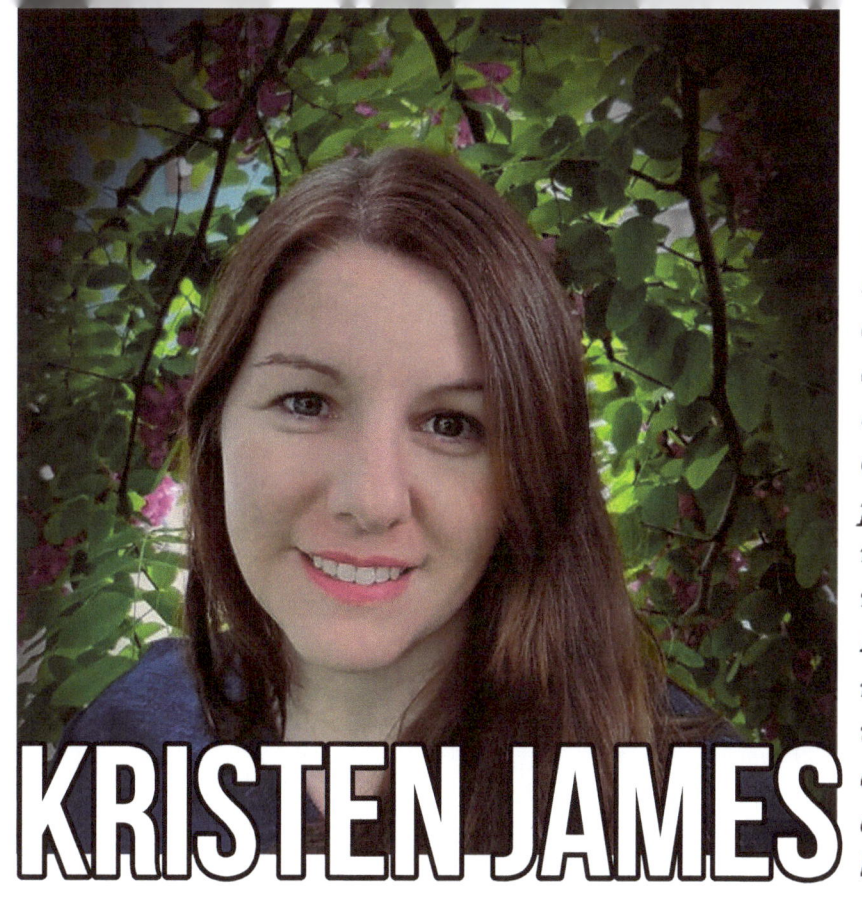

KRISTEN JAMES

Welcome to my world of romance! I've loved reading and writing since early childhood, so my stories have evolved over the last few decades, but I've always included some kind of romance in my stories. My published novels have married romance, second chance, new adult romance, and romantic suspense. My latest release is a billionaire romance that will soon be a trilogy, while I have a work-in-progress about music, love, a little magic, and romance involving a famous lead guitarist.

Some of my stories are a bit different, like Talk to Me, where Avery falls for a voice in her head. I like to mix it up and keep things exciting!

I grew up in the Pacific Northwest and enjoy including the beauty and unique atmosphere of my area in my writing. I've loved the outdoors my entire life and enjoy camping, hiking, and picking wild berries and mushrooms. My hobbies include hula dancing, painting, beekeeping, and gardening--all close to nature! I'm also a business owner and tattoo artist, and I love to travel.

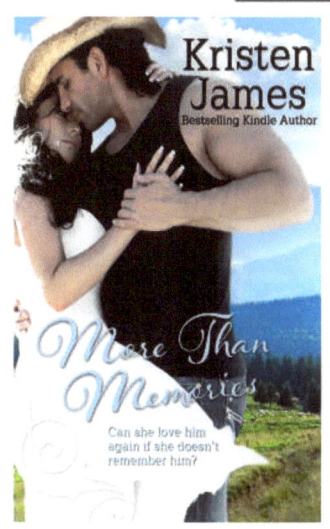
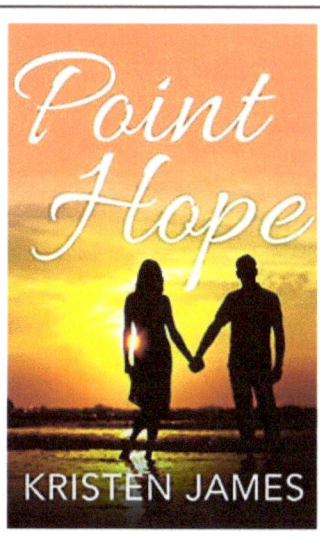
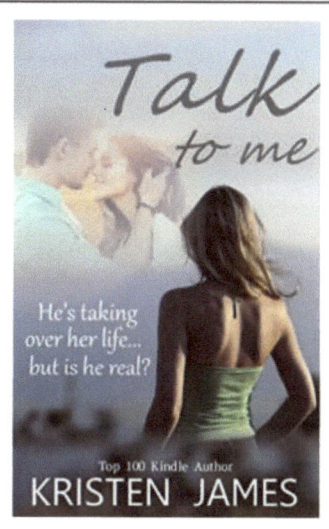
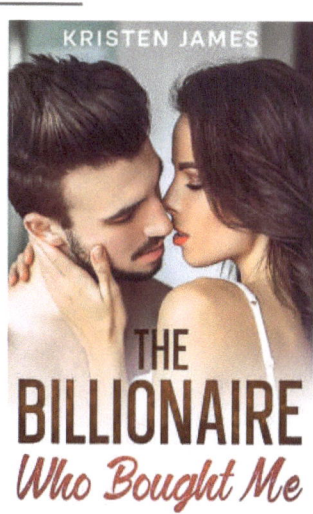

Hearing Ghosts
A Short Story by LONI LYNNE
A Crossroads of Kings Mill Short

Chapter One

Hard to believe she'd finally done it. The struggles of six years of a degree in elementary education with her focus on special education, on top of another two years of receiving her Maryland Certification in American Sign Language. Now she was going to be working her first internship at the Maryland School for the Deaf in Frederick, Maryland.

Since she'd been a young girl in middle school, Kasie Rider had thought of nothing else. She'd given up so much to pursue and focus on just this goal. And now here she was. Standing on the large front porch of the old Victorian home just off of the campus grounds she awaited the Dean of Admissions to stop by and turn over the keys to the newly renovated interns house the school had bought a few years back and restored as temporary housing.

"Hello!" An elderly lady rode up near the front curb on a classic bicycle with a white wicker basket attached at the handle bars and called out cheerfully. "You wouldn't by any chance be Ms. Rider would you?"

"Yes. I am." Kasie stepped a few steps down off the porch as the woman moved her kickstand into place and let her bike lean a bit as she maneuvered off. "Can I help you?"

"I'm Victoria Snyder, a friend of Dean Dorrine Koontz. She told me you would be here by now and that she was terribly sorry but wouldn't be able to meet with you tonight to turn over the keys to you. She asked if I might be able to drop them off and make sure the house was okay for your arrival since I was going to be visiting a friend in the area this evening."

"Oh. That's fine. I appreciate it, Ms. Snyder." Kasie smiled.

"Please, everyone around here calls me Vickie." She walked up to the house and unlocked the old wooden, refurbished door with the skeleton key. "Dean Koontz made sure that everything would be ready. She was so excited for you to be here."

"I don't know why. I'm still an intern." Kasie laughed.

"Yes. But one in which she's hoping you might be able to work with one of her children she's been having trouble with lately." Vickie stated. "She mentioned you had a degree with special education, too."

"I do. But I didn't know she needed me for that."

"Is that going to be an issue?" Vickie went about turning on the lights in the front parlour. "The house was fully refurbished with period antiques. I think it just adds to the ambiance of the old girl. Don't you?"

"It's absolutely beautiful! I noted the copper downspouts and gutters trimming the turret. I can't imagine the cost but it will be beautiful even when it's aged from the patina." Kasie noted.

"Well, it's yours during your internship here at Maryland School for the Deaf so enjoy and take good care of her. And if you need anything, just let me know."

"Thank you so much Vickie. I will. I appreciate your help."

Kasie thanked the elderly woman, who probably had more energy and spirit in her than most young people her own age. She wasn't sure how old she actually was but had a feeling she was older than most people thought. Still, it was nice to have someone check on her who seemed to know something about the school dean and the house.

"He's one of our youngest students but needs a lot of help." Tonya explained as she led Kasie through the hallway of the Maryland School for the Deaf. "Ms. Koontz wants you to work with him one on one, see if there is anything you might be able to help him with."

"So I won't be working with any other children at this time?"

"No, not right now. Ms. Koontz thought it would be a significant start to see what you did one-on-one with Jacob before sending you on to a classroom instruction."

Kasie didn't mind. She was being paid the same and had room and board, she really didn't care. It would be nice to get her feet wet first. Though she had been excited about a room full of students.

The hallway ended. Kasie realized they were in a deserted wing of the school. The echo of their steps dominated the atmosphere. A sense of quiet and unuse surrounded her along with an eerie sense of being watched.

"Here you go. This is your classroom and office for now." Tonya unlocked the old wooden door.

A small room with large windows that faced the row of houses on the street where she lived now, gleamed with a fresh coat of paint, the wooden floors glistened with a new sheen of lacquer. An old blackboard lined one far wall with the American Sign Language finger-spelling alphabet boarding over it. A wooden teachers desk stood in the far corner of the room and small wooden desks with attached chairs, like old time schoolhouse desks, made three smart rows for no more than fifteen students.

"I know it's kind of dated and sparse but just let me know what you need to make the room yours and I'll get it for you." Tonya smiled warmly.

"Thank you. It's charming in its old fashioned way. But yes, I think some colorful warmth to the room, a few plush things for texture to add some softness and welcoming feel would go a long way." Kasie stated. "Perhaps some happy displays of the basic fundamentals up on the bulletin boards."

Nodding, Tonya smiled. "I was thinking that, too. No problem. I will let Ms. Koontz know and we will get them for you. In the meantime, Jacob should be here shortly. Oh, by the way--just a word of warning, Jacob can be a bit flighty."

"You mean disruptive or unfocused. That's natural in any child." Kasie dismissed the issue. She knew kids could be easily distracted, unruly at times, even the best behaved.

"No. I mean flighty. He'll be here one minute and gone the next...physically. He does that. That's why we need you to help."

"What can I do to help that?" Kasie found it rather odd. Would she be chasing this boy up and down the hallway to get him to learn and understand?

"You have the ability to talk to him, on his terms, with his disability. You have a special gift, Kasie. That's why Ms. Koontz hired you."

None of this made sense. Suddenly confused Kasie felt a bit uneasy. Tonya wasn't making much headway.

The other woman laughed. "It's alright, Kasie. You'll figure it all out. You'll be fine, I promise."

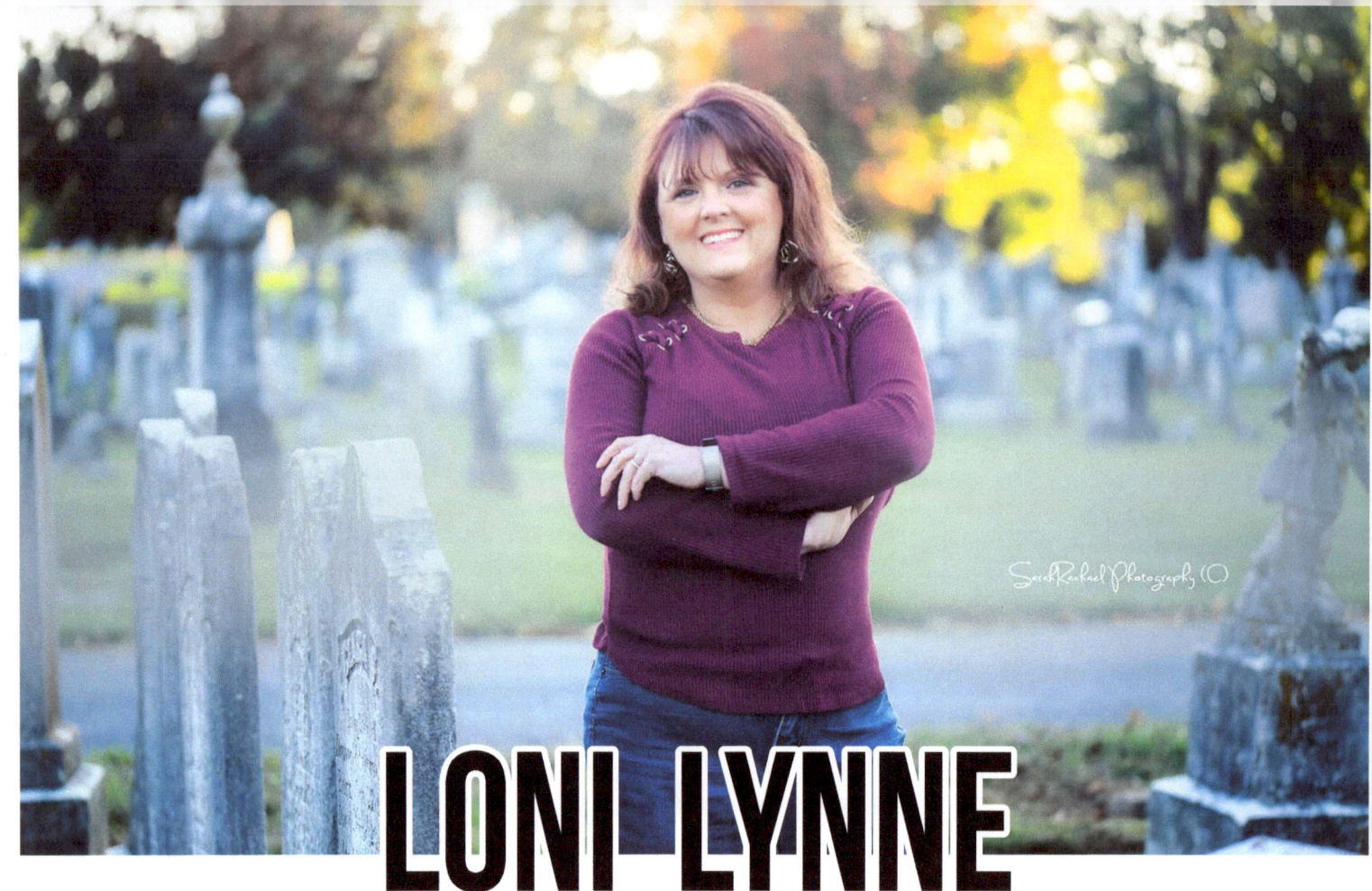

LONI LYNNE

Believe in Fate! Not just her motto, it's Loni Lynne's way of life.

How else could a simple girl born in a small town in central Michigan find herself in western Maryland writing paranormal romance books about Historical (fiction of course) ghosts and shape-shifting immortals from pre-Romanian folklore? It had to be fate.

It might have had something to do with moving every 18 months as a child (oil field brat–not military) or joining the United States Navy when she graduated high school and was sent to Annapolis, Maryland for her first duty station. Or meeting her Annapolitan, Army husband and eventually moving to western Maryland after four years of military honeymooning in Hawaii. Nah...it had to be fate and too many yellow legal pads of half written stories. Whatever it is, Loni Lynne still decides to let fate guide her, her characters and their stories into the hearts of her readers. Because, sometimes you just gotta 'Believe in Fate'.

What makes writing your passion?

It's the ideas that come to me at odd hours. The characters in my head are passionate about needing to come to life. An author breathes that life into them...I love to see where they take me.Katy is a former board member, Spanish spokesperson and workshop facilitator for VOICE Today, a non-profit advocacy for survivors of sexual abuse. She was a model and actor for Real People Models and Talent. Katy is a former member of the Local Advisory Council (LSAC) for Fulton County Schools. She speaks 4 languages and is passionate about inspiring, motivating and helping people.

What's the story behind your choice of characters?

I have two series that I write, right now. Crossroads of Kings Mill are based on historical ghosts (fictional of course). I love working with ghosts and metaphysical characters.
My other series, Guardians of Dacia are immortal shifters who are part of the folklore and legend of Romania in which I had reseached when I was looking up my ancestry on my father's side.

Immortal Heat
GUARDIANS OF DACIA SERIES
by Loni Lynne

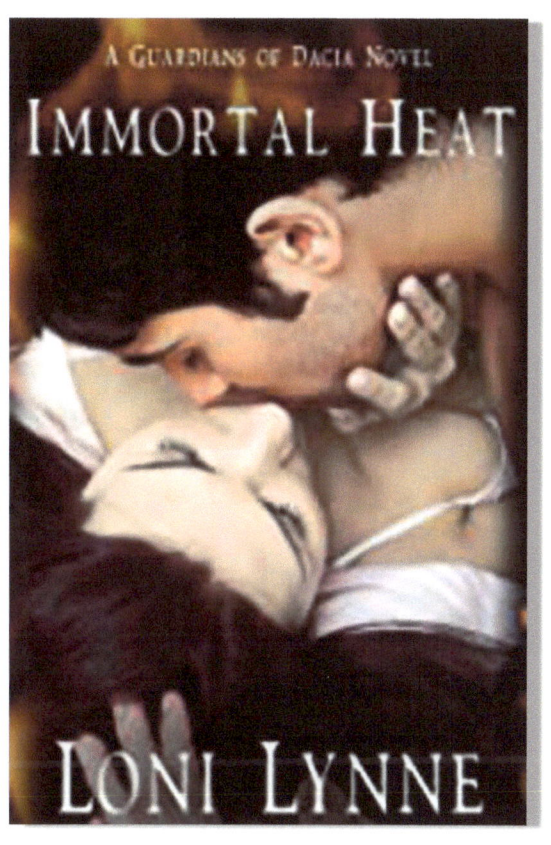

Marilyn Reddlin, can't wait to begin her new life in Cluj-Napoca, Romania. Working with Aiden Vamier, the foremost expert in ancient Dacian History and folklore is a dream come true. She's barely in the country though when a dark stranger warns her to go back to America before it's too late. Too late for what? She has no intention of listening, no matter how intoxicating his voice is or how sexy he looks in black leather--until she's attacked in the airport by a group of vampires.

His only task? Get Marilyn Reddlin to leave Romania. Easy day! A favor to an old friend for saving his life over a thousand years ago, Draylon Conier didn't bargain on protecting her from Aiden Vamier's blood-sucking fiends! This should have been a simple task for the last of the Zmeu dragon-shifters. He could handle one woman. Never had a problem getting them to break a bit. Marilyn Reddlin didn't want to bend, much less break and she let him know. Stubborn woman!

What's so special about her anyway that has both immortal clans playing cloak and dagger? He'll take her to the portal of Dacia, where Rick Delvante and the rest of his immortal clan can keep her safe. If he can. Marilyn Reddlin is the first woman he's met in over a thousand years he can't control, physically or mentally. She's stubborn, independent, beautiful and gods help him, impossible to resist.

Marilyn has just entered a world of danger and secrets based on ancient folklore and legend. Draylon is set to protect her from the powers that be and worse yet, her finding out what he really is. There is no way he will let her be destroyed by Immortal Heat.

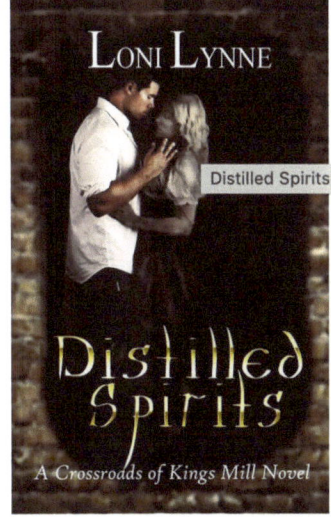
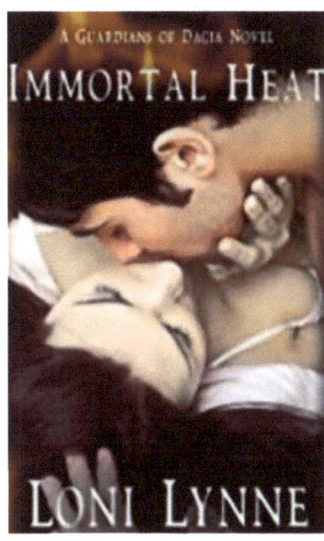
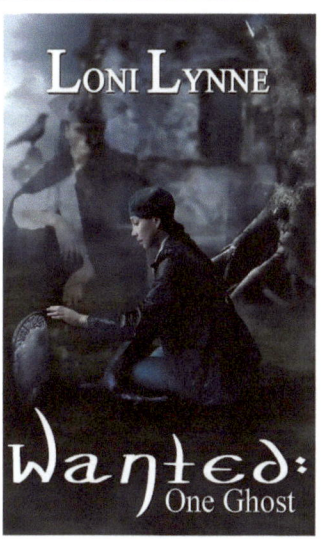

Jody Hadlock

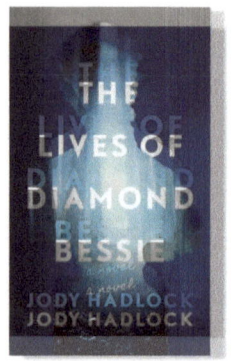

Jody Hadlock's love of history goes all the way back to junior high, when she was a member of the Junior Historians of Texas, so it's no surprise her first novel is historical. She studied journalism at Texas A&M University and worked as a broadcast journalist and then in nonprofit public relations before turning her focus to fiction. She also writes screenplays and won the 2020 Dallas International Film Festival's screenplay contest.

"This affecting tale of a 19th-century American woman struggling to prove her worth other than as a marriage prospect leaves a lasting impression." Publishers Weekly

The Lovely Bones meets the Wild, Wild West in this haunting tale inspired by a true story.

Pregnant out of wedlock, sixteen-year-old Annie Moore is sent to live at a convent for fallen women. When the nuns take her baby, Annie escapes, determined to find a way to be reunited with her daughter. But few rights or opportunities are available to a woman in the 1860s, and after failing to find a respectable job, she resorts to prostitution in order to survive.

As a highly sought-after demi-mondaine, Annie—now Bessie—garners many expensive gifts from her admirers and eventually meets and marries the son of a wealthy jeweler, a traveling salesman with a gambling problem. With her marriage, she believes her dream of returning to proper society has finally come true. She's proven wrong when she suffers the ultimate betrayal at the hands of the man she thought would be her salvation. But Bessie doesn't let her story end there.

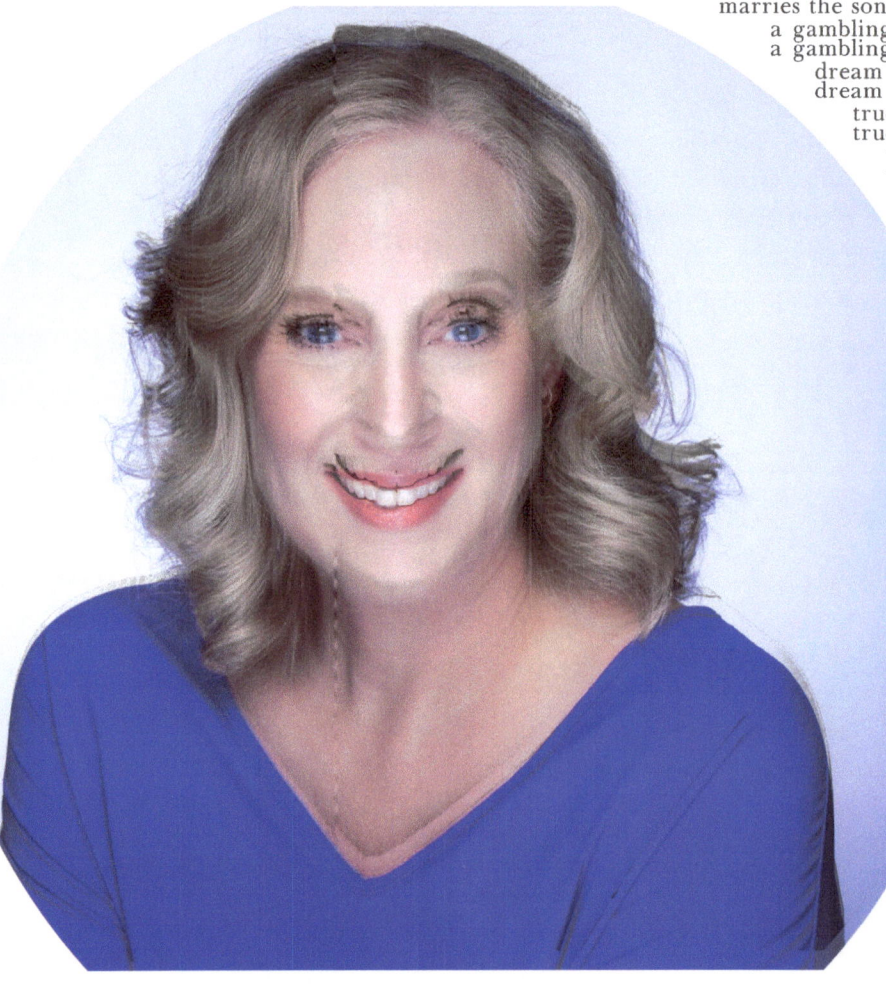

Set against the backdrop of the burgeoning women's rights movement, The Lives of Diamond Bessie is a captivating tale of betrayal and redemption that explores whether seeking revenge is worth the price you might pay.

"As fascinating as it is riveting as it is original, The Lives of Diamond Bessie is a compelling novel of historical suspense. Bessie is a character who will haunt you for all the right reasons—for her determination, her heart, and her soul. I was enthralled." NYT bestselling author M.J.

JOY HARDING

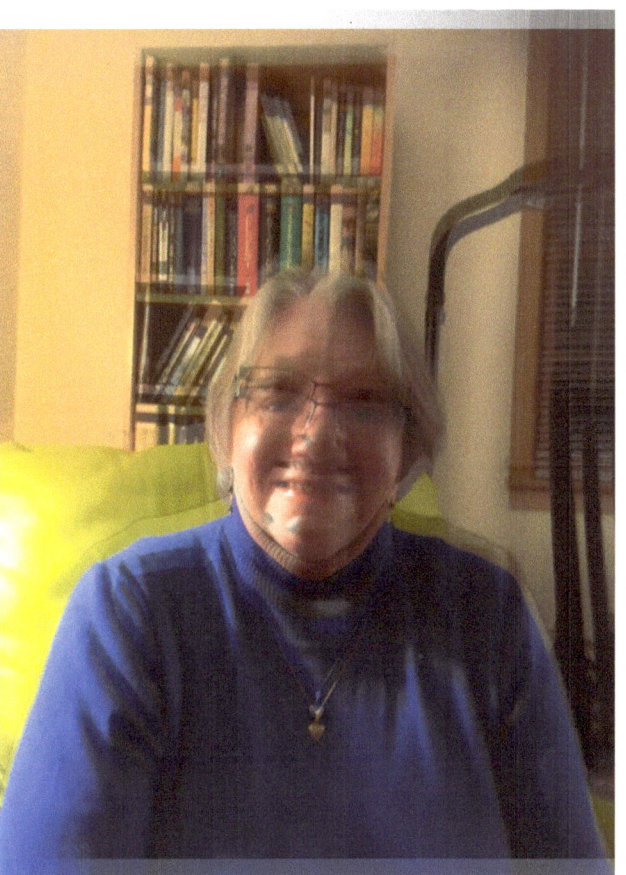

Joy Harding is a Christian, a wordsmith, and a lover of books. She is committed to bringing you, her readers, exciting journeys, uplifting love stories, and family sagas that will touch your hearts. Together with her husband of almost 40 years, Joy is a passionate believer in the centrality of God in their covenant marriage relationship. Her characters reflect this passion through good times and bad.

Trained as an attorney, Joy lives in the beautiful state of Minnesota. Her first series, Boundary Waters Search and Rescue, is set in the northwoods of her home state.

Joy loves to hear from her readers.

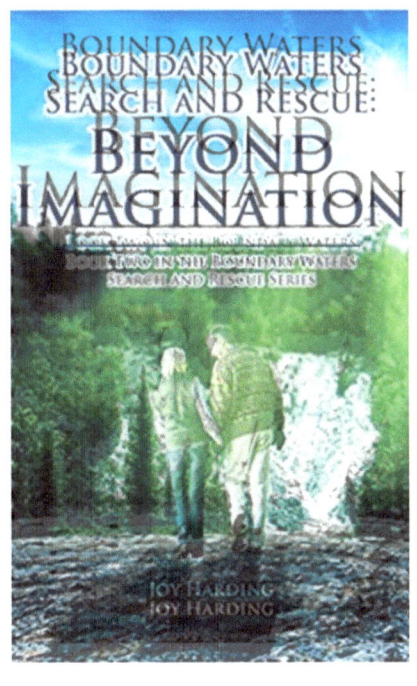
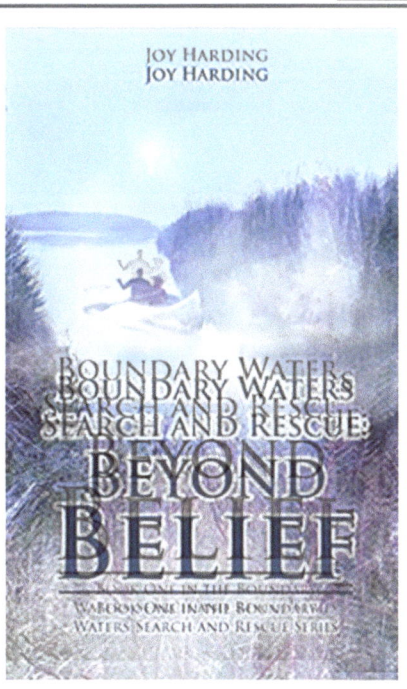

GLENN GOODWIN

Author Glenn Goodwin has lived an exciting life with all types of twists and turns, ups and downs. Much more than any of the characters he has penned about. While being diagnosed with dyslexia at age six, school was a struggle. He later had to beat a rare and deadly form of cancer at age 17. As time went on, Glenn obtained two master's degrees in education and business. After he had to make a career change, Glenn started over from scratch. He has lived and taught in various countries around the world, inspiring many along the way that they can live their dreams and do anything as long as they grind. One of the sayings he lives by is, "Adversity builds character, and with that, anything is possible despite the adversities." His book embraces all aspects of life and struggles a person could face and get inside your head and think, let alone feel. The book and characters have a bit of everything as well as many twists and turns you will not see coming.

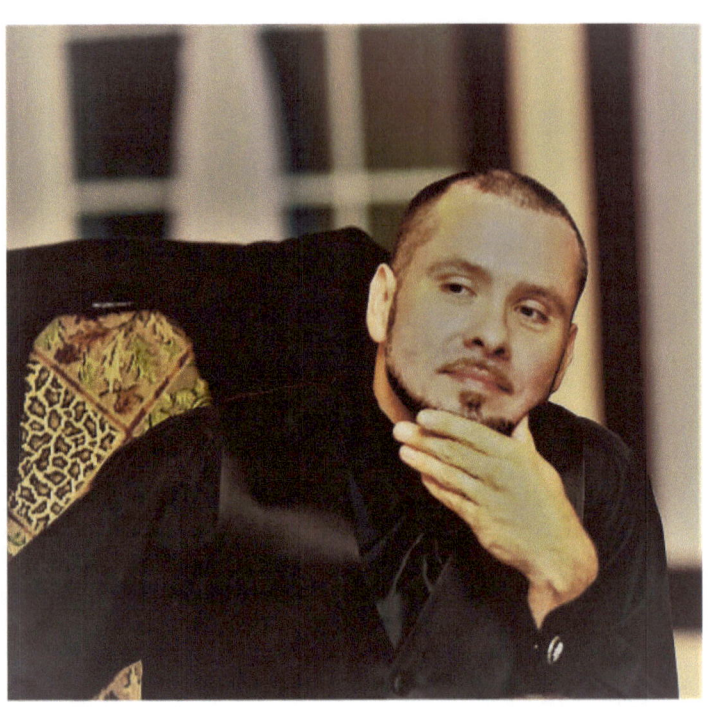

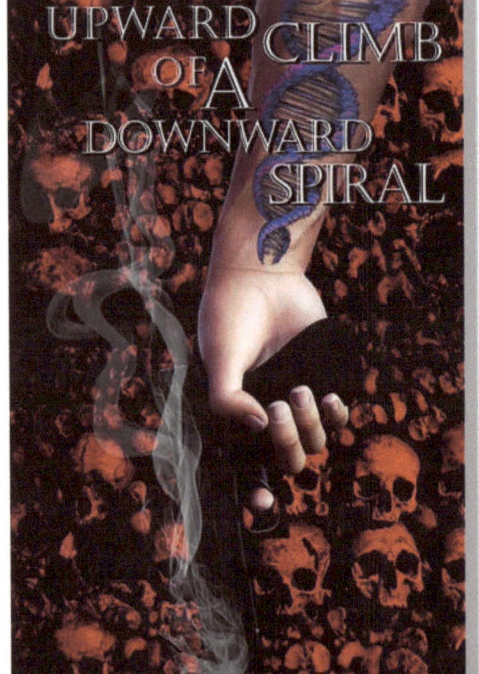

Can a wronged heart that bleeds pain, conflict, and a thirst for revenge, ever be righted?

What price would you pay to get everything owed to you while losing everything you have?

These are just two of the questions one man must find the answers to in the hell he helped create. Embracing the evil lurking within, even his own dark shadows are beginning to frighten him. While welcoming a lifestyle born in the depths of society's insatiable thirst for corruption, Gunner walks a tightrope of questionable actions. Caring less about the answer to those actions, Gunner knows he's possibly damning his soul and the lives of those he loves as he presses on. Will he lose his mind and soul? Eventually giving into absolute power, crime, and unspeakable addictions; forgetting about love and what he has lost. Or will he rise through the ashes settling all scores while setting the world on fire just to watch it burn? Only Gunner knows what he must do… despite the cost!

JOSIE MALONE

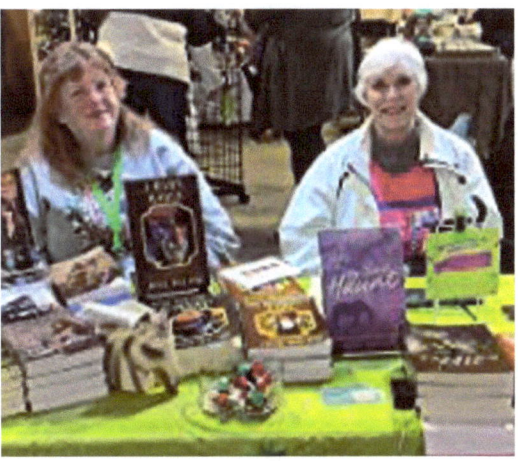

I live on the family farm, a riding stable in the Cascade foothills. I organize most of the riding programs, teach horsemanship, nurse sick horses, hold for the shoer, train whoever needs it – four-legged and two-legged. And write books in my spare time, usually from 8PM to 2AM, seven days a week after a long day on the ranch.

When I can't write, due to the overwhelming needs and pressures of the "real" world, words and stories fill my mind. Even when I muck the barn, I think about books or short stories or pieces in progress and map out the writing in my mind. My newest project is the next book in my Liberty Valley Love series. I'll have a new release in the Baker City Hearts and Haunts series in June 2022.

I have 19 horses to look after, along with other assorted animals here on the farm. I'm teaching the kids and grandkids of the ones I taught way back when we started. I've had a lot of adventures over the years, and I plan to write all about them. I hope you enjoy reading about them!

I am a member of the Evergreen Romance Writers of America chapter and the Writer's Co-Op of the Pacific Northwest. I have B.A. degrees in English and History, and my master's in teaching degree.

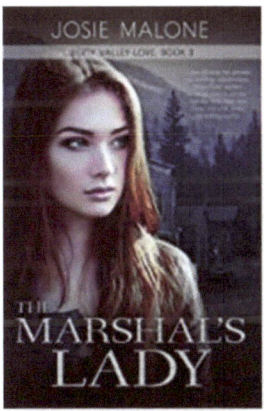
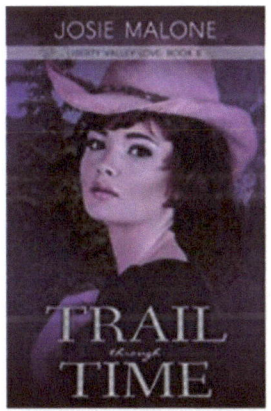
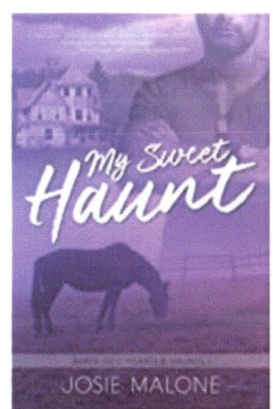
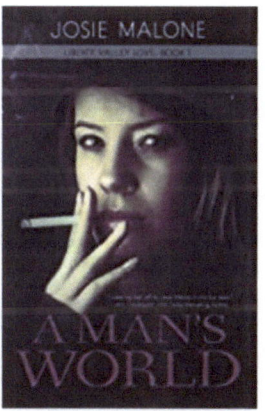
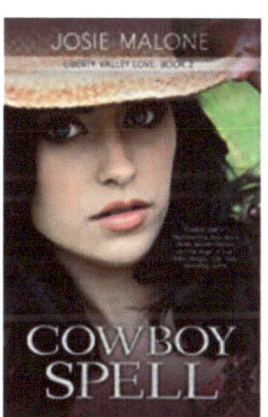
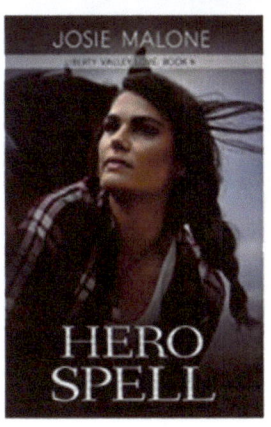
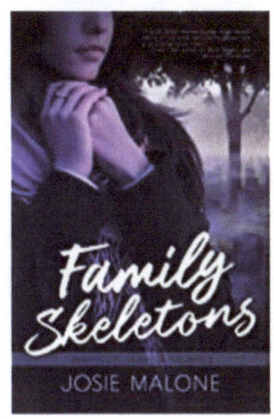
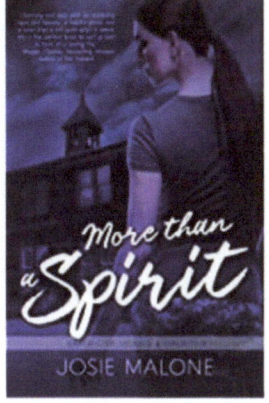
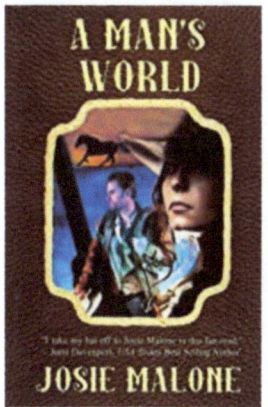
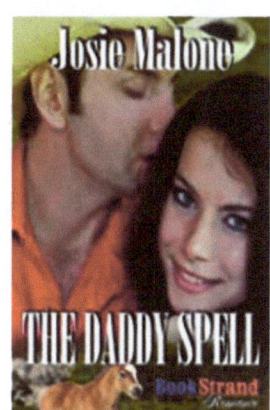

SHELDON SHALLEY

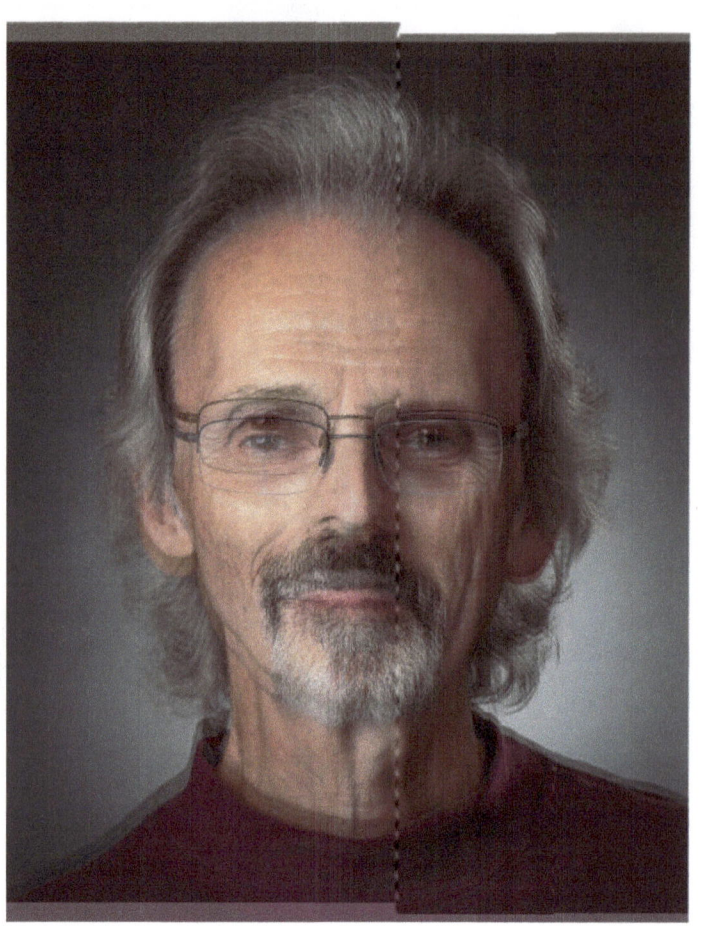

I am a psychotherapist, clinical social worker, educator, artist, shamanic practitioner and author. My personal psycho-sexual-spiritual journey and work as a psychotherapist for 30 years have given me direct experience with healing the emotional, psychological and spiritual wounds or human suffering.

My book, The Other Man in Me, is the story of my journey of discovering into the symbolic and spiritual meaning of my erotic longings and sexual attraction. On the journey I met another man living in my soul; one that connected me to the meaning and purpose of my life and helped me make peace with my masculine and feminine selves.

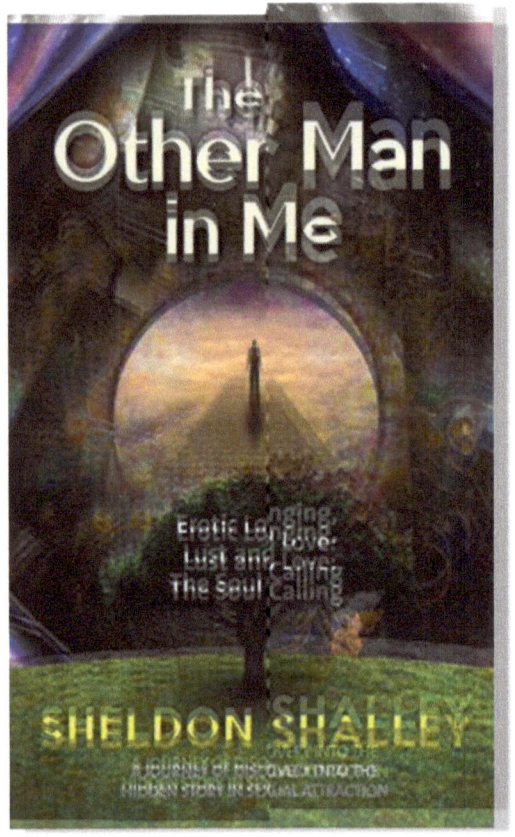

THE OTHER MAN IN ME
Erotic Longing, Lust and Love: The Soul Calling

The Other Man in Me is the story of one man's journey to understand his bi-sexuality and how to reconcile his two selves—the one attracted to women and the one attracted to men and the responsible husband, father, church and community leader and the one caught in brief same-sex encounters and affairs. Drawing from both personal and archetypal material presented in his dreams, fantasies, spontaneous images arising in meditation, his art and exploring same-sex motifs found in mythology and customs and rituals of some indigenous societies, The Other Man in Me tells the story of the discovery of the symbolic and spiritual meanings of same-sex attractions.

MELISSA CYNOVA

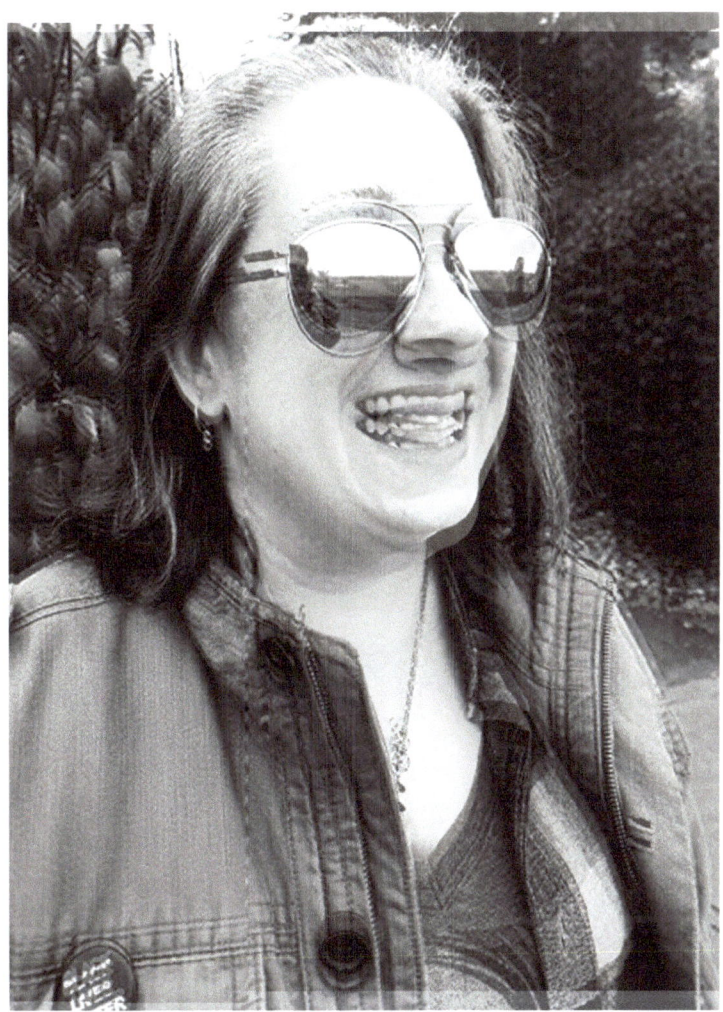

Tarot cards are pieces of paper with a series of symbolic art on them. That's it.

Tarot READERS, though, now there's some magic.

I've been reading tarot cards for 30 years (well, 29.5 technically) and I can tell you that they're not magical, mystical or otherwise. The cards are cards, and you're the one who makes them amazing.

My first book, Kitchen Table Tarot, provides a down to earth, common sense approach to reading tarot cards. It also won the Independent Publisher Award for Best First Book, so that was cool.

My second book, Tarot Elements: Five Readings to Reset Your Life, is coming out in the spring of 2019, and gives you five readings to help you unstick yourself in the home, heart, mind, body and soul.

I live in St. Louis with my husband, Joe (who is my favorite), my kiddos and four black cats, two dogs, and our tortoise, Phil. I really, really like superhero movies and when I'm not reading or writing, I'm hanging out with my friends. I'm a lucky girl.

I'm working on a tarot deck with artist, Cate Anevski, another deck with my friend Ellie, and have outlines for two more books. You can reach out to me for tarot readings at www.melissacynova.com

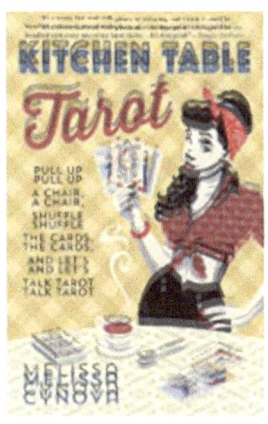 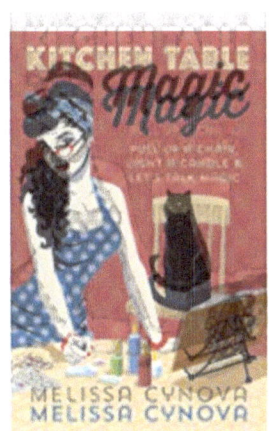 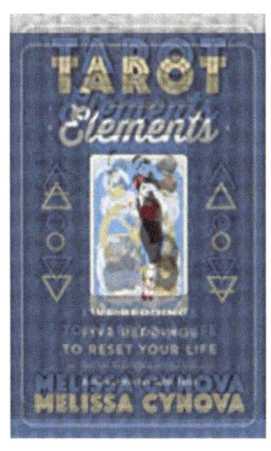 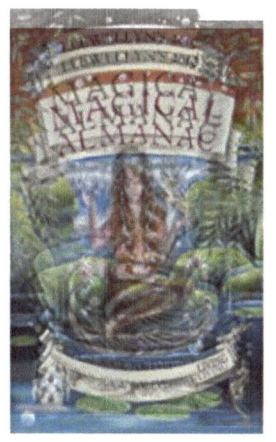 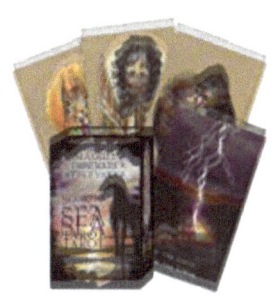

KITCHEN TABLE MAGIC
Pull Up a Chair, Light a Candle & Let's Talk Magic

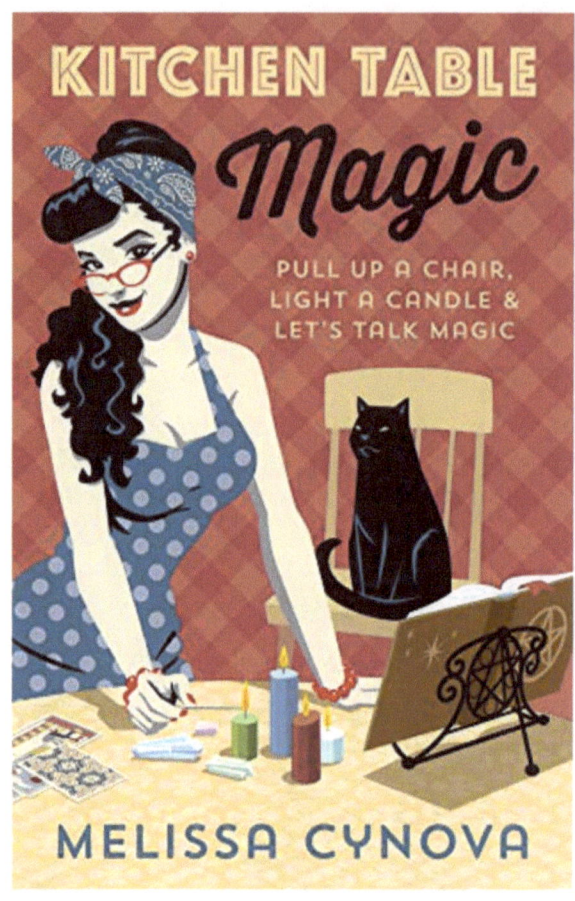

Discover Your Inner Magic with a No-Nonsense Teacher at Your Side

This beginner's guide to magic is like sitting down at the kitchen table with Melissa Cynova as she shows how to use simple prayers, spells, and rituals to make positive improvements in your life. Melissa's straightforward and witty style makes it easy to start working magic for love, luck, prosperity, protection, blessings, and more. With tips for setting intentions effectively and connecting with spiritual energies in a safe way, Kitchen Table Magic is a perfect first step on a magical journey. You will also learn how to use gemstones, crystals, pendulums, tarot cards, and other tools that will enhance your spell work. Magic has been used by people around the world for thousands of years. This book is a down-to-earth guide to powerful and effective magical techniques for connecting with spirit and creating the life that you truly desire.

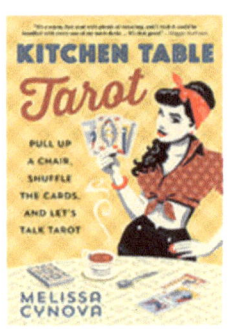 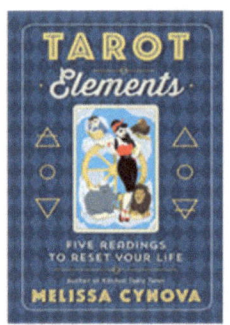 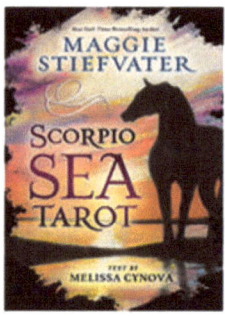

Melissa Cynova, bestselling author of Kitchen Table Tarot, provides a magic starter kit that is perfect for beginners. In her down-to-earth, no-nonsense style, Melissa shows how to use magic in dozens of different ways to help make positive improvements in your life and in your community. You will discover how to set intentions and goals, how to safely work with magical energies, and how to work magic for love, luck, prosperity, protection, blessings, and much more.

Magic has been used by people from many different religious or spiritual backgrounds for thousands of years. This book shares tips and techniques for simple prayers, spells, and rituals that can make a major difference in the world. You will also discover important guidance on magical ethics, as well as hands-on instructions for working with gemstones, crystals, pendulums, tarot cards, and all sorts of tools that will help you achieve your magical goals.

T. L. SCOTT

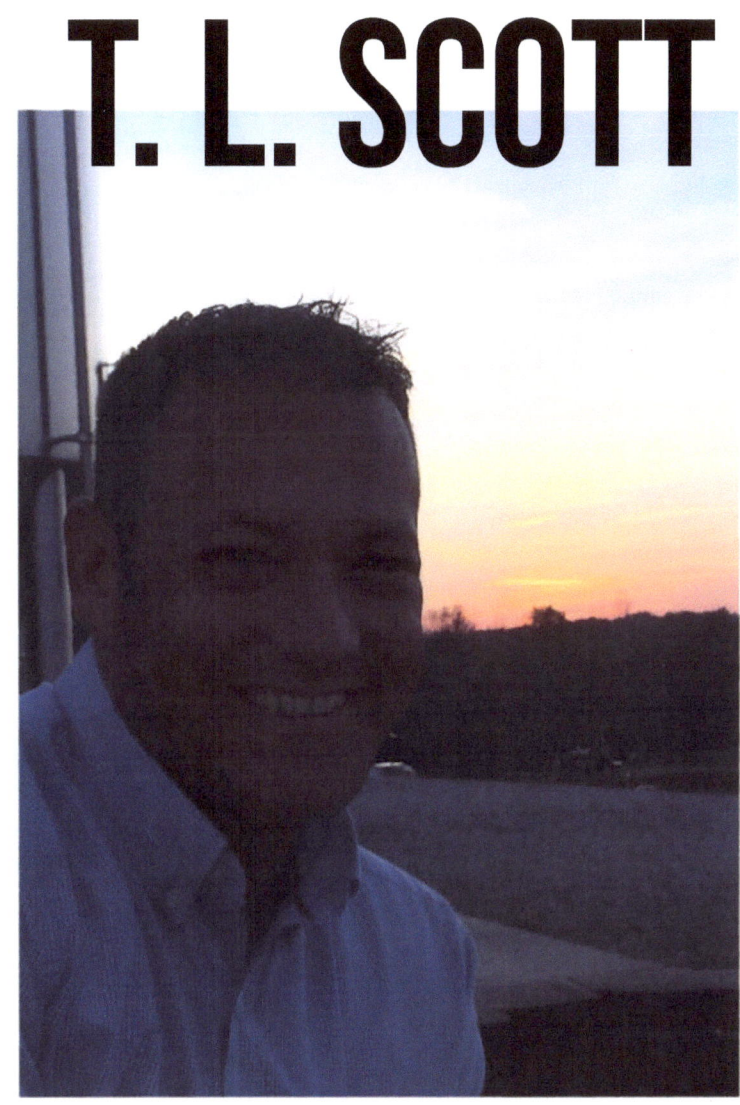

Hi,

I have just completed my fifth novel, the second in the series, titled Shifting Sands. It will be up on Amazon this week. This series is a crime fighting series. Bill, an ex-Army special forces operator now FBI Agent is on the trail of Miguel, the leader of a criminal network involved in drug and human trafficking. Bill is assigned to the task force to bring him and his gang to justice.

Since retiring from the US Navy I have been able to invest the time required to bring my stories to life. I have always been an avid reader and now I am able to enjoy the process of bringing stories from the original inspiration to the full blown story. I love the process and I love that I can share these stories with others.

I look forward to talking with you more.

T. L. Scott

TL Scott grew up in a small mid-western town. He could often be found with his nose in a good book, even while walking around. Small town life was good but he craved adventure. He wanted to make a difference with his life so he joined the Navy. Over the course of his Naval career, Scott was exposed to people from all walks of life. It is from his love of storytelling and passion for characters of all types that give his characters life. They are the ones that tell their story.

Scott's break-out novel A Life Worth Living is a tale of a families struggles with love and loss. Dave and Debbie have grown distant from each other while trying to juggle successful careers and two children. When tragedy strikes they must decide how much they are willing to sacrifice to make theirs A Life Worth Living.

His second novel, Fault Line, follows Bill and his buddies. They are visiting his hometown while on leave from the war. Bill's baby sister is getting married. The soldiers are forced into action when they cross the path of a gang that has invaded this idyllic western town. There is no way this gang could have settled in so deep without help. Someone had to have helped them. Someone has crossed the line, the Fault Line.

His third book, Levels, was released in November of 2018. Jake discovers he has the ability to cross over to other realities. He has to stay alive and learn to control this ability while he fights to find his way back to his normal. He discovers that others have abilities of their own. Together they team up to fight the enforcers in a battle that is much bigger than they know.

His fourth book and second of the Levels series, titled Tunnels follows the adventures of Jake and Clare. They have both grown in their abilities since that day at Wentley's department store. This time they face their greatest enemy. Billions of lives hang in the balance across reality after reality.

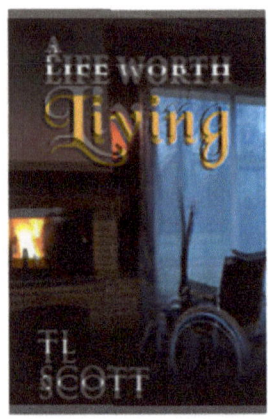

T. L. Scott's breakout novel is a family drama that tells the story of Dave, a hard-working man who has made sacrifices for his family. All he wants to do is provide a good life for his family. He sacrifices his time with them to provide them the lifestyle he believes they deserve. When tragedy strikes, he is forced to face the consequences of his decisions. How hard will he have to fight? How much will he be willing to sacrifice to hold onto the life he has? This is a story of love, loss, and one mans struggle to find redemption. It is a story of how far one man will go to make his a Life Worth Living.

A Life Worth Living is a story that has a message that resonates in today's hectic world where so many families have dual bread earners, struggling to make ends meet. Fans of Nicholas Sparks, Danielle Steele, and Luanne Rice will love A Life Worth Living.

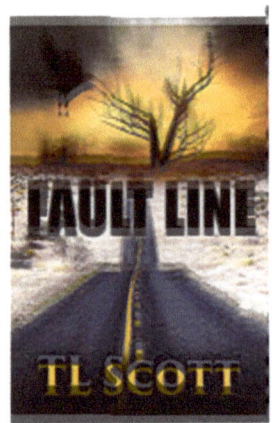

Bill has come home to see his little sister get married. He brought along some of his Army buddies to enjoy this slice of small town America. They were looking forward to getting some rest and relaxation away from war. Unfortunately, war has found them here, on the streets of small town America. This tranquil setting is interrupted when a man forces a woman down on her knees in the middle of Main street. When he brings the muzzle down, just inches from her beautiful face, the soldiers are forced to take action.

This fast-paced novel has the soldiers teaming up with local law enforcement and agents from the FBI to eradicate a gang that has invaded the very fabric of this town. They couldn't have become so embedded without help, help from someone in a position of power, someone that is at fault and has definitely crossed the line, the Fault Line.

MORE BOOKS BY T. L. SCOTT

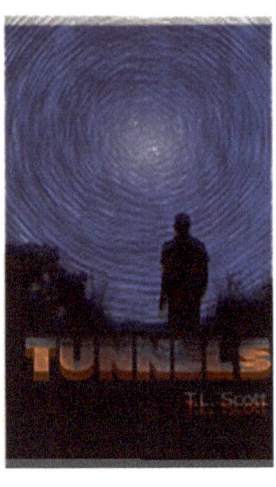
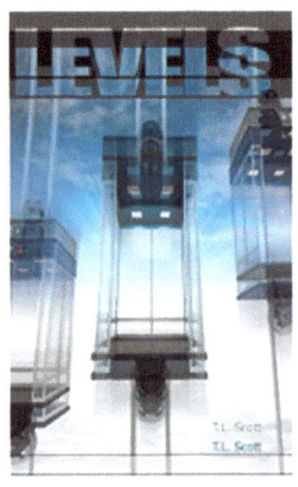
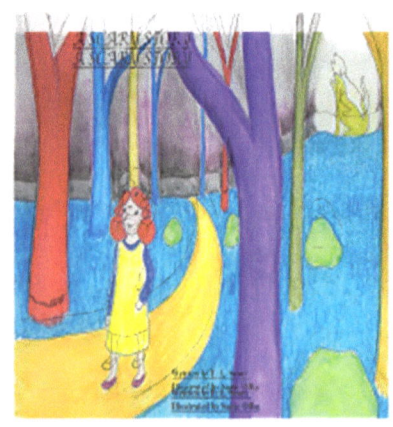
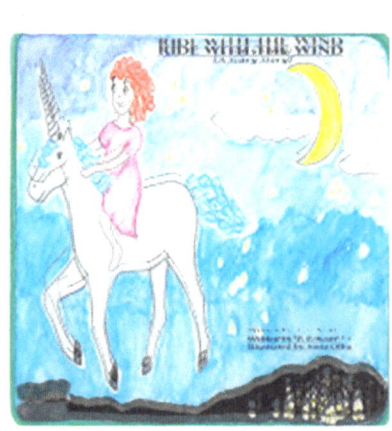

DK Marie

DK Marie's a voracious reader. Her number one love is romance and devours any and all of its genres, but also enjoys thrillers, horror, and non-fiction. Basically, if there are words on a page and a spectacular story, she's diving in, heart and soul.

However, there's one thing she loves even more, and that's writing her own steamy contemporary romances. They're a mixture of heart, heat, and humor. Brimming with confident heroines and kind heroes, all living, loving, and lusting in and around her hometown of Detroit, Michigan.

When not falling in love with her characters, DK Marie is laughing, relaxing, and planning her next adventure with her family. Okay, and also drinking boatloads of coffee, chatting on social media, and dreaming about her next travel destination.

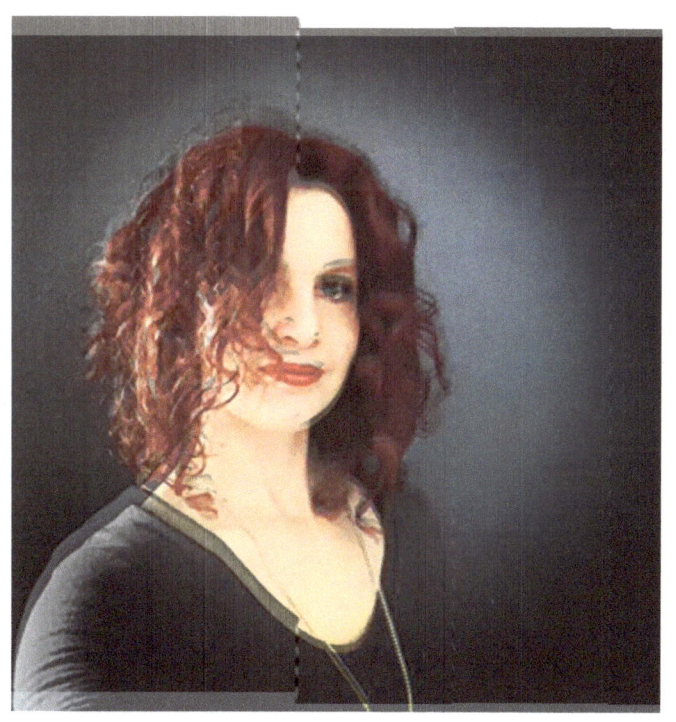

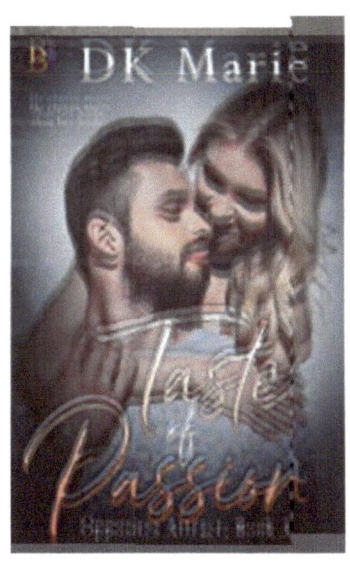
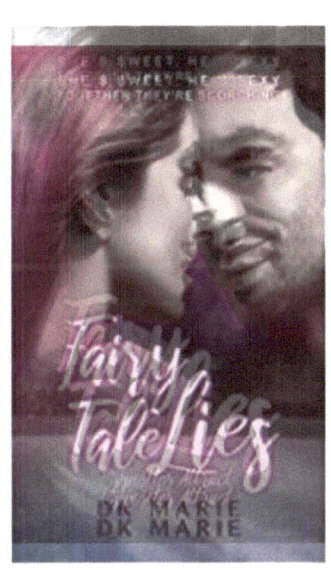
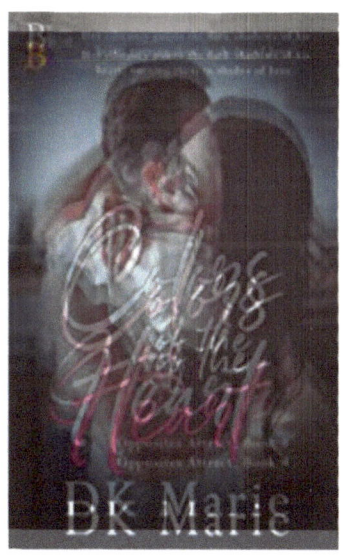
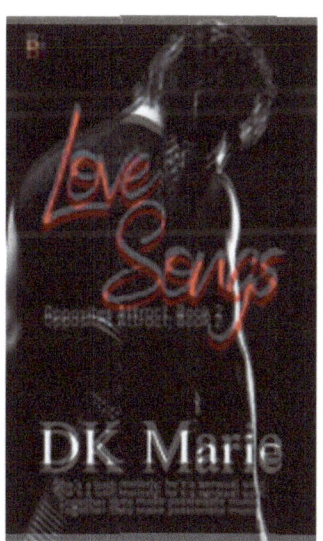

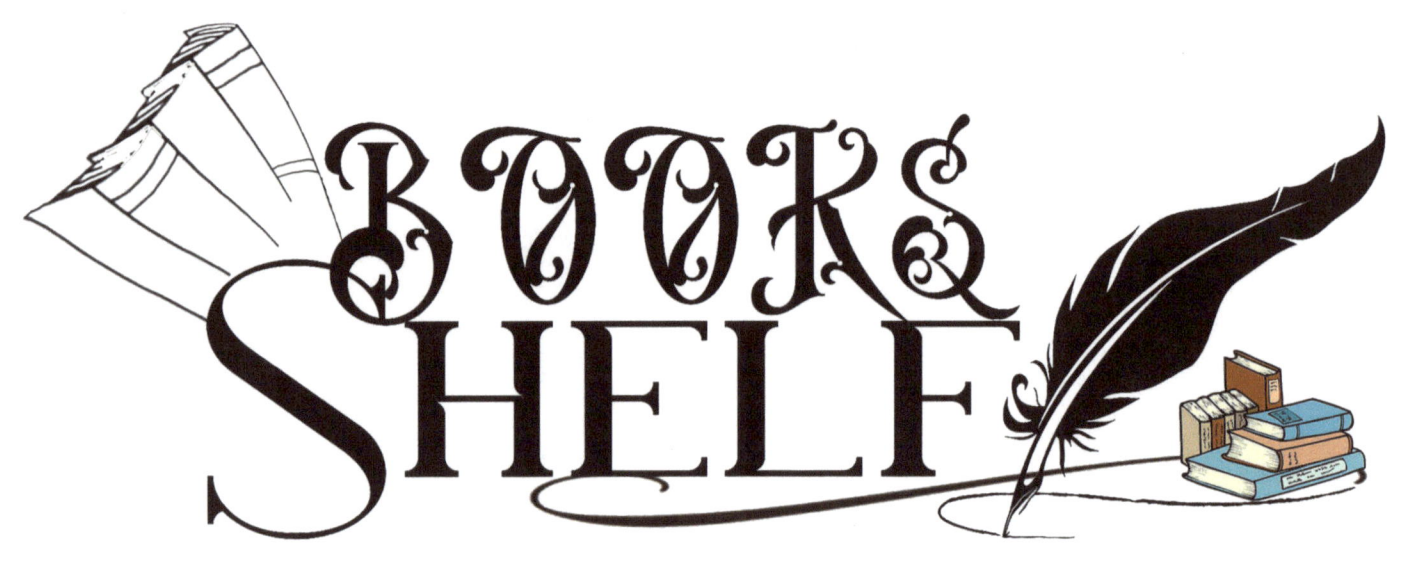

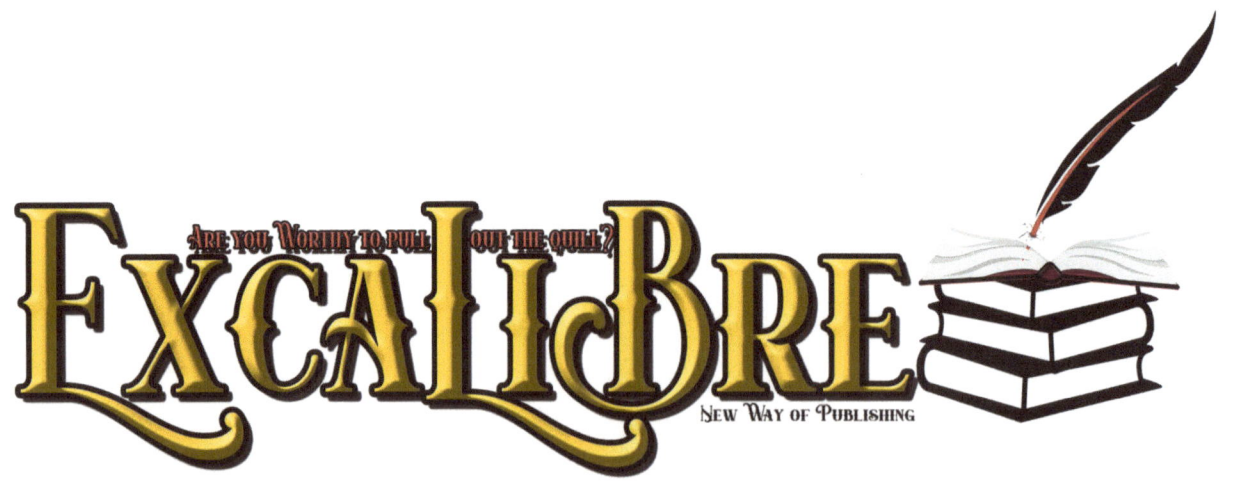

www.ingramcontent.com/pod-product-compliance
Lightning Source LLC
Chambersburg PA
CBHW051936210526
45473CB00006B/2265